D0609147

036395

CREATING DEMAND

POWERFUL TIPS AND
TACTICS FOR MARKETING
YOUR PRODUCT OR SERVICE

CREATING DEMAND
POWERFUL TIPS AND
TACTICS FOR MARKETING
YOUR PRODUCT OR SERVICE

Richard Ott

Edited by Martin Snead

BUSINESS ONE IRWIN
Homewood, Illinois 60430

This publication is designed to provide accurate and authoritative information in regard to the subject matter covered. It is sold with the understanding that neither the author nor the publisher is engaged in rendering legal, accounting, or other professional service. If legal advice or other expert assistance is required, the services of a competent professional person should be sought.

From a Declaration of Principles jointly adopted by a Committee of the American Bar Association and a Committee of Publishers.

Sponsoring editor: Jeffrey A. Krames
Project editor: Gladys True
Production manager: Ann Cassady
Jacket Designer: Phil Kantz
Compositor: Publication Services
Typeface: 11/14 Palatino
Printer: Arcata Graphics/Kingsport

Library of Congress Cataloging-in-Publication Data

Ott, Richard (Richard Alan)
    Creating demand : powerful tips and tactics for marketing your product or service / Richard Ott ; edited by Martin Snead.
      p.   cm.
    Includes index.
    ISBN 1-55623-560-7
    1. New products—Marketing.   I. Snead, Martin. II. Title.
HF5415. 153.088 1991   91–13212
658.8—dc20

Printed in the United States of America
1 2 3 4 5 6 7 8 9 0 AGK 8 7 6 5 4 3 2 1

For Charles, Genevieve, Henry, and Jeanne

Preface

Most people think of demand as an uncontrollable, obstinate force that comes and goes as it pleases. Like the Dow Jones Industrial Average (which is really only the aggregated buy/sell preferences of millions of individuals), demand is often thought of as a powerful living organism with a mind of its own. "What did the Dow do today?" one might ask. Similarly, people are always asking questions like "Is demand increasing or decreasing?" or "Is there demand for this product?" or "What is demand likely to be for kloptigobinators over the next 10 years?" Demand is viewed as a "given" in the equation, affecting all the other variables–including the lives of products, companies, and individuals.

Here are two better questions you can ask right now. "Is demand really such an independent, unpredictable force, or can the marketer* exercise some control over it?" and "If it can be controlled, what can I do to create, grow, and sustain demand for my product (or service) in a major way?"

You'll have the answer to the first question before finishing this Preface. The answer to the second question encompasses the remainder of the book.

---

*The term *marketer* refers to anyone formally or informally involved in the production and mass selling of a product, service, or oneself. Whether you're the chairman of the board, a marketing manager or sales manager, a small business owner, a self-employed professional person, a politician, a job seeker, or anyone else interested in influencing the masses, you're a marketer.

WHAT CREATING DEMAND *ISN'T*

When I told a friend of mine the name of this book was going to be *Creating Demand*, he said "hmm...sounds manipulative." If it sounds that way to you, let's set the record straight now.

In a capitalist society, the consumer is king. Everything is done for the benefit of consumers. Consumers determine what will be supplied by how they choose to spend their dollars. And make no mistake about it, consumers choose to spend their dollars as they please. They make the final decision to buy or not to buy. They are the ultimate authority. They are in charge.

One of the underlying assumptions you must accept to be a successful marketer is that the public cannot be "manipulated." No matter how clever you are and how much money you spend, you cannot exercise any mind control over the public and "make" people buy your product or service. Oh, I know the world is full of crooks and con artists who are seemingly able to fleece the public with one crazy scam after the next. Even some legitimate marketers with legitimate products sometimes delve into the gray area of deception at times. But such practices usually don't work en masse (you can only fool some of the people, not all of them), and most have flash-in-the-pan longevity (you can't fool people for very long and continue to get away with it).

Marketers that rely on some degree of "manipulation" always end up with poor sales, bad publicity, angry customers, or all three. Some end up out of business, or in jail—neither of which falls into the success category.

WHAT CREATING DEMAND *IS*

First, demand creation is a concept. It's a new way of looking at demand, based on the beliefs that (a) demand is not an uncontrollable, incorrigible force, and (b) demand can be governed to a large degree by the marketer. It puts the marketer in a *proactive* position to affect demand, rather than merely a *reactive* position to be indiscriminately affected by demand.

Second, demand creation is the active application of sophisticated psychological techniques aimed at inducing desire and action in individuals. In that sense, the marketer creates demand the same way a comedian creates laughter. Both laughter and demand are inherent desires of every human being (people want to laugh and they want to consume). When a comedian is funny, he induces laughter in his audience. Since people like to laugh, they like the comedian and they like what he does to them. When a marketer applies the right psychological techniques, she induces desire (for the product or service) in her audience. Since people like to consume, they like what the marketer does to them, and they react by purchasing the product or service.

Third, creating demand involves the correct use of powerful marketing strategies and techniques that leverage desire and action to the masses. When you, the marketer, understand why and how these marketing methods work, you can actually create major demand for your product or service.

Demand creation goes far beyond the old approaches of simply recognizing and serving demand ("let's find out what people want and give it to 'em"), and stimulating demand ("let's tell people about our product and the benefits they'll get from it"). Demand creation involves a lot more than advertising, though advertising is a major ingredient. When you're creating demand, you're operating at the high end of marketing sophistication. You needn't be concerned about the relative complexity of its underlying theory, however; I've explained it all in simple, easy-to-understand, step-by-step fashion.

To get to the level at which major demand erupts, however, you first have to master certain marketing fundamentals. Therefore, I stress fundamentals in the first portion of the book, lest I be guilty of sending you off in a jet that hasn't been properly built or maintained.

HOW THIS BOOK WILL HELP YOU

There's so much information on marketing floating around, it's difficult for even the most seasoned marketers to get a handle on it. Many marketers are downright misguided and confused. They're snowed under by the mountain of material, most of which is confusing and contradictory to begin with. As a consequence, a marketer often doesn't even know where to begin or what to do after he has taken the first step.

I saw the need for one definitive source that boils it all down, that edits out all the irrelevant knowledge and presents only the essence. A book that simplifies, not complicates. A book that includes procedural steps so you know exactly how to implement what you learn.

So I've gathered and sifted, evaluated and condensed, organized and structured. Some of the material in this book is brand-new, cutting-edge. Some of the material is classic—the accumulated wisdom of the ages. But all of it is extremely powerful and essential for any marketer aspiring to the highest levels of success in the 90s and beyond.

Most of the material in this book has universal application, regardless of business type or size. The strategies and techniques will work for you, whether you're a one-person entrepreneur just getting started, or a top-level executive with a multinational conglomerate, or anywhere in between.

It will be up to you, however, to mold and adapt the material to your own particular situation. Although I don't know what industry you're in, or what your product or service might be, I do know this: You have the ability to create ideas and implement them effectively. You may need someone to set up the parameters, point you in the right direction, and fire the starting gun, but that's what I'm here for. The rest is up to you.

Keep a pen and a pad of paper with you as you read each chapter. If an idea of how you can use a particular technique suddenly comes to mind, put the book down and write away! Some ideas may come to you at unusual times—in the middle of the night, for example. Do not let an idea or even a random thought slip by without jotting it down. Go ahead and implement the idea, too, if the time is right. You don't have to finish the book before acting. You can create and implement as you go along.

IT'S TIME TO PUSH THE GO BUTTON

If you're ready to move ahead, I'm ready to guide you along. Hang on to your seat... we're about to make your demand jet soar!

Richard Ott

Acknowledgments

This book would not have been possible without the assistance of Martin Snead. Martin not only contributed much of the material, but expertly and painstakingly edited the entire manuscript (many times over).

I'd like to thank Jeff Krames, Gladys True, Kate Wickham, and the entire Business One Irwin staff for their invaluable guidance and support—and my researcher, Susan Miller, who I'm convinced can find the answer to any question at all in less time than it takes most of us to phrase the question.

The following people also deserve mention for their assistance: James Gartner, Janet Taylor, Kim Pavkovich, Lindy Snead, Joe Kylman, Troy Bryant, and Nita Burns.

Contents

A new method of programming your advertising to reach and affect people on two different levels of consciousness.

A cutting-edge secret to incredible advertising impact that works whether people are paying attention to your ads or not. Equally remarkable: it costs you no more than what you're already spending on advertising!

PART 5   SUSTAINING DEMAND

Using the seeds of each success to feed subsequent successes is what *parlaying* is all about.

One of the best techniques for sustaining demand is *reinforcement*. How to keep your demand fire from burning out.

Avoiding the five pitfalls that can destroy demand.

PART 6   GETTING HELP

How to get the most out of your agency.

There is one ingredient necessary to make the material in this book work. It is something that you, the marketer, must supply.

PART 1

SETTING YOURSELF UP FOR SUCCESS

Before you delve into the sophisticated range of high-powered demand creation, you must have a solid foundation of basics in place. Otherwise, all the sophisticated stuff won't work. Amazingly, marketers often have no problem executing the sophisticated techniques, even as they simultaneously drop the ball when it comes to the basics, thereby rendering their entire marketing effort ineffectual.

As a management consultant, I deal on a daily basis with all kinds of marketers who are seeking help in one form or another. Guess what? In three quarters of the cases, it's the basics that I deliver. Only 25 percent of all marketers are ever ready to deal with anything beyond the basics. And those that are ready always "check off" on the basics first anyway.

Chapters 1 through 4 are about setting yourself up to succeed going in. They will provide you with a solid foundation on which to build your marketing program and create the massive demand you desire.

Chapter One

The Prerequisites
of Demand Creation

R ecently, I met with some very nervous owners of a CHR-formatted* radio station in a medium-sized city. The station had enjoyed high-flying success for many years, but lately they were getting killed in the ratings by a new CHR competitor. They felt the time had come to take some new and decisive measures to regain listenership. They wanted to discuss the possibility of retaining my firm to help. (Although my management consultancy works with companies in a variety of industries, most of our business is with radio and television stations. In broadcasting, the object is to increase ratings. The use of consultants is very widespread in broadcasting. Just about every radio and television station has at least one of us on the payroll.)

The meeting was a real experience. Within 15 seconds of walking into their building, I was briskly escorted down the hallway, past peeking eyeballs behind cracked doors, into a hushed "war room," where five of their top executives anxiously awaited. After a round of introductions on their part and a quick travel synopsis

---

*CHR stands for "Contemporary Hit Radio," called "Top 40" in the old days.

on my part (clients find great assurance in knowing the consultant has traveled long and far to get to their city), they began to pick up their chairs. The president of the radio division suggested we all huddle in the center of the room and speak in whispers, presumably (I gathered) to foil any cup-holding eavesdroppers behind the door or in the ventilator shaft.

For the next hour, they proceeded to tell me everything one would ever want to know about their main competitor. Speaking in military terms, they not only gave me the blow-by-blow of how the competitor "blindsided us" with a "flank attack," but they recounted every promotional stunt the competitor had ever pulled. They were especially incensed by the recent discovery that the competitor had been stealing their trash and combing it for memos. "They kept coming on the air with the exact same promotions and contests we were planning!" one of the executives declared.

Although I did find their war stories somewhat entertaining, eventually I knew it was time for me to step in and redirect the conversation. I had to get their attention off the competitor, first of all. Second, I had to focus their attention on what really matters initially: accurately assessing their own ability (or inability as the case may be) to succeed.

YOUR FIRST PRIORITY

Specifically, I wanted to find out if they had the three *prerequisites of marketing success* in place. If they did, I knew I could help them succeed in getting their listeners back. If they didn't, I knew they had to get the three prerequisites in place or nothing else they did would matter. *Without the three prerequisites of success in place, success is simply not in the cards.*

The three prerequisites of success are musts for all marketers, including you, regardless of the industry you're in or the nature of your product or service. They are your first priority in demand creation.

In addition, the prerequisites of success form your main fortress of defense. When you have all three in place, you're well-insulated against competitive moves, whatever they may be. If you lack any one of the prerequisites, you're vulnerable. If you lack any two, it's only a matter of time before you fall victim to a competitor. If you lack all three, you're already dead.

As we discuss each of the prerequisites of success, evaluate your own position. If you are deficient in one or more of them, please spend your time and effort acquiring the ones you don't have or beefing up the ones you do. Once you have the three prerequisites solidly in place, you'll automatically leap to the top 20 percent of all businesses in the free world . . . and that's even before you begin to market!

PREREQUISITE NUMBER ONE: YOU MUST ADOPT A MARKETING MINDSET

It doesn't matter whether you are the chairman of the board of a multinational corporation or the sole proprietor of your own small business. It doesn't matter whether your current job title includes the word "marketing," "advertising," "promotion," or anything even remotely close. It doesn't even matter if you have any prior marketing experience. If you want to create demand (even if you won't be handling the actual duties), *you* must first adopt a marketing mindset.

What do I mean by a marketing mindset? A marketing mindset is composed of four elements:

1. You must *acknowledge the importance of marketing.* Marketing is, or will be, responsible for a large degree of your success. And it will become increasingly so in the 90s.
2. You must *appreciate the marketing process.* Marketing—the primary elements of which are advertising, promotion, publicity, and contesting—employs some fascinating psychological principles and exciting media usage techniques. At least it's fascinating and exciting to those in tune; be one of them, and you'll have lots of fun along the way.
3. You must *respect the people who create and execute.* Although *you* are the one who must adopt a marketing mindset, you

may not be the person who does all the marketing brain-
work and legwork. You may have people to do that for you
in your company. And you will certainly have people outside your organization helping you, including the media
people you deal with and any creative/production suppli-
ers or ad agency people. A healthy display of respect and
appreciation goes a long way.

4. You must *remind yourself of the importance of marketing, your
appreciation of the process, and respect for the people—daily.* You
must *think marketing* all the time (not every minute of every
day, but at least once a day).

You can always tell when people do not have a marketing
mindset in place. They're always in scramble mode, as though
they wake up one morning and realize they've got to mount some
sort of ad campaign by the end of the week. Also, people without
a marketing mindset tend to be in a perpetual state of frustration
and disappointment. They never really understand why things
aren't working.

Without a marketing mindset, you'll never get your marketing program off the ground. You'll be constantly fighting with
yourself and with any colleagues who *do* have a marketing mindset. Or you may not give much thought to marketing at all. And
you'll certainly give in to the strong and recurring temptation
to cut your marketing expenses. Without a marketing mindset,
you'll end up sabotaging your own marketing success time and
time again.

PREREQUISITE NUMBER TWO: YOU MUST BE
COMMITTED TO DEVELOPING A QUALITY PRODUCT

The quality of your product or service must be high. Obviously.
Yet as obvious as it seems, an amazingly high number of marketers seem oblivious to it.

The real problem is that each legitimate marketer *believes* his
product is of high quality, whether or not that is really the case.
Thinking he has that base covered, he spends little energy ques-

tioning and testing his own quality. The radio station I spoke of earlier was putting out such a bad on-air product it deserved to lose listeners. It certainly wasn't going to attract any more listeners until the product was improved considerably. And don't forget what got domestic car manufacturers into trouble. Prior to the 1980s, General Motors, Ford, and Chrysler hadn't even heard of the word quality.

So how is your product's quality? You need to answer that from the viewpoint of your customer or consumer, not your own viewpoint. Every so often, you should pull yourself away from the day-to-day workings of your particular job and physically go out into the marketplace. Talk to consumers or your customers. Observe what they do. Evaluate your product vis-a-vis the other alternatives available to the consumer. How does your product stack up? Is the quality really there?

Quality is not as subjective as most people believe. The public has a remarkable ability to ascertain quality, and usually rather quickly. People may debate the value of product differences— Ford has its loyal customers and so does Chevrolet—but people seldom debate quality. That's one reason some products sell steadily year after year and others disappear as rapidly as they appeared.

When you don't have a high-quality product or service (relative to its price category), you stand to waste a lot of money attempting to create significant demand. As we all know, the best marketing in the world won't help a poor-quality product.

In years past, under the Pillsbury ownership, Burger King kept hiring and firing new ad agencies and mounting new ad campaigns with rapid succession. Each go-around produced no greater sales than the previous one. Wasn't it obvious to them that advertising was not the problem? Either none of the Burger King executives actually ate at their own restaurants, or their closeness distorted their ability to conclude that room-temperature burgers and apathetic counter clerks constituted subpar quality. As is often the case with marketers that mistakenly pay poor attention to product quality, they eventually gave up and sold the chain. Actually, the entire Pillsbury company, including Burger King, was acquired by Grand Metropolitan in 1989. What was Grand Met's first priority? Improving Burger King's product and service quality.

One other thing: Quality can fluctuate. Sometimes you're ahead of the competition; sometimes they jump ahead of you. Sometimes your product works without a hitch; sometimes a bug appears. Notice, however, the way this prerequisite is written. You must be *committed to developing* a quality product. Your commitment to quality should not waiver. If you are truly committed to having a high-quality product, on average, you'll have it.

PREREQUISITE NUMBER THREE: YOU MUST HAVE MONEY

You must have money to spend on marketing, or you won't be doing much of it. You can't afford to waste time griping, moaning, and complaining about the expenditures. Nor can you afford bringing on heart attacks or ulcers every time you sign another check. No question about it . . . marketing costs money. Accept it and move on. That's the bad news.

The good news is that (a) you can probably save a good chunk of your present expenditures by eliminating waste and inefficiencies, and (b) you can make the dollars you do spend pay off big. (We'll discuss it all in subsequent chapters.) Your payoff can be so big, in fact, that your return on investment is nothing short of phenomenal, well worth every dollar you put in.

Say I offered you this deal: Take a $50 bill out of your wallet or purse right now and set it down in front of you. I'm going to step up and take that bill, put it in my pocket, and keep it. Then I'm going to pull a $100 bill out of my pocket and give it to you in return. Would you do that deal?

Of course you would, provided you had a fifty in your possession to begin with. And provided that it was available to invest in this deal and not preallocated to something else.

Is it unrealistic to think you could realize a 100 percent return on your marketing investment? Probably. Most successful marketers realize far *greater* than 100 percent returns. According to *Advertising Age*, the top 100 advertisers in 1989 together averaged

$61.28 in sales for every dollar they spent on advertising.* That's a 6,128 percent return on investment. And that's just the average. Many do better. Of course, other factors besides advertising affect sales, but the point still holds: Marketing—including its largest component, advertising—can pay off big. This book will guide you through all the right moves to make for a big payoff, but you have to supply the money to do the job.

How Much Money Do You Need?

The actual amount of marketing money you need is relative. Relative to the size of your business, the industry you're in, the level of competition, and what you're trying to accomplish, just to name a few variables. In 1989, Philip Morris generated $44.759 billion in revenue with advertising expenditures of $2.07 billion.† That same year, Kimal Lumber Company of Venice, Florida, generated over $10 million in revenue by spending $5,092 on advertising. Many successful companies spend vastly different amounts on marketing.

How much should you allocate to marketing? I wish I could spare you ambiguity, but the real answer is that you need enough money to do the job. No more, no less. No matter what you spend, however, you'll be able to put it to good use by implementing the techniques in this book. Almost all are designed to produce the highest possible results with the least amount of expenditure. Some even cost very little to implement.

Time Is an Alternative

What if you simply do not have any marketing money? Does that mean you're destined for failure? Not necessarily. There is a substitute for money, and it's called time. If you don't have the money, then you'd better have the time.

Advertising Age, September 26, 1990, page 2. Reprinted with permission.
†*Advertising Age*, September 26, 1990, page 1. Reprinted with permission.

Thompson's Drapery Company, the Richmond, Virginia, decorating company that did the "window treatments" in my house, has more business than they can handle. Their phones never stop ringing, and the money's rolling in. Yet they never spent over $1,500 on marketing in any one year. But they've been in business for over 37 years, the first 30 of which the phones weren't ringing nearly to the degree they have been in the last seven years. If you don't have marketing money, you'd better have a lot of time. A *lot* of time.

This book is primarily for marketers that aren't fortunate enough to have decades in which to build demand slowly, however. Most of the techniques contained herein are designed to boost demand rather quickly. If that's what you have in mind, and you've got the three prerequisites of success in place, you're ready to move ahead.

Chapter Two

The Power Tools of Marketing

T he Crazed Complicator inhabits small and large companies alike. He believes that the marketing of his product or service is, or should be, a Byzantine and convoluted process. Every working day is dedicated to that belief. With research grinding and computer whirling, the Crazed Complicator (who goes by the title of Director of Marketing or Advertising Manager or the like) presides over a self-perpetuated mountain of information. From that perch the Crazed Complicator directs a plethora of swirling advertising and promotional maneuvers with such vigor, a Hartsfield air traffic controller would appear comatose by comparison.

The prime by-product of the Crazed Complicator is disorganization and confusion. Internally, few co-workers understand what is going on, though they may have some appreciation for the Crazed Complicator's dazzling style. Out in the marketplace, people are definitely confused. But the Crazed Complicator keeps throwing so many new ads and promotions out there that some do take effect. Despite his drawbacks, the Crazed Complicator can maintain a moderate degree of success, at least until upper management discovers how fast he's chewing up the budget. (Interestingly, I've seen a few Crazed Complicators raise their own stock by purposely creating confusion. By making it appear that marketing is an overwhelmingly complex endeavor, a Crazed Complicator can sometimes snow upper management into believing he is the only person capable of dealing with the "enormity" of it all.)

LET SIMPLICITY BE YOUR PHILOSOPHY

You don't want to be a Crazed Complicator. Nor do you want to be intimidated by some Crazed Complicator who tries to make you feel inferior because you choose not to welter in complexity.

There is a much better approach. Its basis is simplicity. The idea is to whittle marketing down to a few easily managed parts. You then forget about the shavings and concentrate on becoming good at managing those few important parts. Let's whittle.

THE NON-TEXTBOOK DEFINITION

The textbook definition of marketing, which goes something like "all commercial activity that gets a product or service from the producer to the consumer," is very broad. Our definition of marketing is much more focused: persuading the masses to buy.

The difference between marketing and sales is in the masses. Sales is primarily a one-on-one function, salesperson to prospect. Marketing uses the media and other vehicles to reach and persuade many people—people who may not ever have any direct contact with someone from the marketer's company.

MARKETING'S FOUR PRIMARY COMPONENTS

Let's take our definition of marketing—persuading the masses to buy—and whittle it down further. The task of persuading the masses becomes a lot easier when we deal strictly with marketing's four primary components: *advertising, promotion, publicity,* and *contesting.* These four components of marketing are the tools you will use to market your product or service.

As we discuss each tool below, note the relative emphasis placed on each. For example, you should devote roughly 50 to 60 percent of your marketing resources (attention and money) to advertising. You may be surprised by the emphasis some of the tools command.

TOOL NUMBER ONE: ADVERTISING

I define *advertising* as the purchase of exposure in mass media outlets. (This includes the production of ads and commercials as well as the buying of media time and space.) A media outlet is an individual radio station, television station, magazine, newspaper, or the like. (Print is a medium; newspapers are media; *The Washington Post* is a media outlet.)

About 50 to 60 percent of your marketing resources should be allocated to advertising. It is your number one tool in demand creation. That's because advertising has two big advantages:

- **Advertising is controlled by the marketer.** You control not only the message, but also the level of exposure.

- **Advertising has the potential to reach and affect mass numbers of people quickly.** When done correctly, advertising can produce tremendous results in a relatively short period of time.

Advertising's biggest drawback is that it costs money—sometimes big money—to reach the level at which results kick in and the ad expenditures pay off. As I mentioned in the last chapter, there are two ways of making your expenditures pay off big: cutting wasted spending and improving each ad's effectiveness. Chapter 4 is devoted entirely to cutting waste (not only in advertising, but in all areas of marketing). Beginning in Chapter 5, you'll find numerous techniques, some with incredible power, to boost the effectiveness of your advertising.

TOOL NUMBER TWO: PROMOTIONS

A promotion (noun) is an event requiring attendance and/or other kinds of participation on the part of the public (or your customers). A contest is a promotion, as a truck is a vehicle. But not all promotions are contests, as not all vehicles are trucks.

Contests (tool number four) warrant their own category, so we'll discuss them later.

Promotions should garner about 20 to 30 percent of your marketing resources.

There are three types of promotional events: *self-sponsored, cosponsored,* and *ride-along.* Each differs based on the role or degree of sponsorship, the marketer assumes.

Self-sponsored promotions are events you create, organize, execute, and finance yourself. Say, for example, the owner of a gift shop has an open house one weekend. Or a radio station puts on a raft race. Or a soft drink holds "taste tests" around the country. Or Kool cigarettes organizes a jazz festival. These are all examples of promotions in which the marketer assumes the role of sole sponsor.

Cosponsored promotions, sometimes called partnership promotions, are events in which two or more marketers join together and assume equal sponsorship roles. Each marketer brings its expertise and money to the table, and each shares in the benefits. For instance, McDonald's and NBC got together for the "McMillions" contest first run in the fall of 1990. Or a radio station and a night club might throw a party. Or a newspaper and a shopping mall could cosponsor a business show. If you've noticed in these examples, the optimum combination of copromoters is when one is a media outlet and the other has high-traffic physical locations.

Ride-along promotions are events sponsored by another party, but in which the marketer participates. In many cases, the participating marketer may pay a fee to the sponsor(s) in exchange for involvement. In some cases, the marketer simply trades product for involvement. If a florist rents booth space at a fair or trade show, the florist is riding along on the fair or show. A soft drink distributor rides along when she gives away product at an auto dealership's grand opening. A television station rides along when it has a float in a local Christmas parade.

TOOL NUMBER THREE: PUBLICITY

Publicity is defined as nonpurchased exposure in the news, editorial, or noncommercial section of a media outlet's material.

Publicity should get about 5 to 10 percent of your marketing resources. Since publicity, by definition, is nonpurchased exposure, your dollar expenditures on it will go to creating and disseminating information about your product or service.

Shouldn't publicity warrant more than only 5 to 10 percent of your resources? Hey, everyone wants publicity. It can certainly do wonders for those marketers that are successful in getting it. But some very funny things can happen as a result of its pursuit. Perhaps the "gobs of wonderful publicity" you were hoping for will turn out to be but a token mention in some generic fashion. For example, the newspaper article might report on the big, citywide clothing drive by noting "a thousand dollars worth of brand new leisure wear was donated by *a local clothing merchant*" (that's you!)

Or a feature story about you in the local magazine finally comes out, and lo and behold, you can't believe your eyes! How could that nice reporter who spent three whole days as your best buddy write such a scathing exposé? Not only does the story rip you to shreds, but they used an unflattering photo of you in a goofy pose that was taken as part of the "test" shots before the "real" shots were supposedly taken!

Or one of those syndicated television tabloid shows gets ahold of a document you should have shredded, a tape you should have erased, or an ex-employee you shouldn't have crossed, and in one day's time you go from a low-profile, out-of-court settler to a high-profile, nationally known bonehead.

Or you got lucky and received a good amount of coverage in a positive vein. This happens about 20 percent of the time.

You're Out of Control

Unlike advertising, which the marketer controls, publicity is totally out of control of the marketer. The newspaper, magazine, or radio or television station granting the publicity is in total control. Reporters and writers can say almost anything they please about you or your company. If you're a "public figure," they can even go so far as to *make up* things about you that may have no basis in reality.

When a marketer becomes a "victim of negative press," she often reels into shock or befuddlement. "How could this happen?" she wonders incredulously. She may get angry and attempt to retaliate. Canceling one's advertising on the offending media outlet is the usual response, though some people take it further, with lawsuits and other veiled threats.

I experienced such an incident in the early 70s, when I was a disc jockey in Lansing, Michigan. The guy who did the news during my airshift led his 3:30 P.M. newscast with a story on a local car dealer that was caught turning back the odometer on used cars. Not the biggest news event ever to hit Lansing, but it must have been a slow news day. Anyway, the newsman delivered the story like it *was* the biggest news story of the year, complete with such phrases as "caught red-handed" and "ripping off the public."

Well, guess who was the sponsor of the newscast? That's right, it was the car dealer. As the newsman finished the odometer story, he paused and said "more news after this," a standard line going into a commercial. I fired off the commercial, and there's the owner of the dealership himself talking about his wonderful selection of low-mileage used cars.

The next thing I know, Mr. Low Mileage is on the phone screaming louder and faster than he did in his commercials, and using a lot of expletives that I didn't recall as part of his commercial vocabulary. I told him this was the request line and I'd be happy to get a song on for him; otherwise he'd have to call the business office—which he must have done, since we never ran his commercials after that. (The usual radio station salesperson's stance on such an incident is to point out to the client that he needs even *more* commercials now to counteract the ill effects of the hatchet job.)

Understanding Why

The question I'm asked most often about publicity is, "What can I do to get favorable publicity and prevent negative publicity?" Let me answer by first pointing out my position. I speak as a marketer, a consultant to many other marketers, and as a former member of the media (including radio news reporting, writing, and anchoring). I take no sides, but explain it from both sides.

First, you should understand why negative publicity exists as often as it does. Here are the reasons:

- **A media outlet may be uninformed or misinformed.** A writer or reporter needs information, but it won't necessarily be all the information you'd like them to have. Do not assume any media people know about you or all the goods things you're up to. It's not incumbent upon the media to seek out favorable information about you; it's incumbent upon you to provide them with favorable information.

- **The marketer and the media have different, and often opposing, goals.** The marketer is focused on getting favorable media exposure, but the media couldn't care less about that. The media want to disseminate information that (a) tells people something they don't already know, and (b) affects as many people as possible.

  All marketers think their activity warrants major exposure. I've found that it's almost impossible for most marketers to understand how few people they are really affecting, or how little the public at large cares about the marketer's activity. It may have taken three years of struggle and your entire life's savings to open your very own restaurant, but believe me, no more than a handful of people really care. It may be the biggest thing in your life, but it's not the biggest thing, or even of any consequence at all, to 99.9 percent of the population at large.

  If that's difficult for you to accept, look at it from the consumer's point of view. If you ranked all of the things that are important in your life right now, where would you rank toothpaste? Is toothpaste of such importance that you give it more than a passing thought, if that? A toothpaste producer might be spending $20 million a year on advertising, and might employ hundreds of people in its production and marketing departments, but is that of any consequence or concern to you? Even if you're a dentist, I doubt that toothpaste occupies more than one billionth of your interest at any given point in time.

That's why barely half of the eligible voters in the United States vote in presidential elections. Even something as important as electing our president is an unimportant element in many people's lives.

When a media outlet denies you publicity, it's probably because they're evaluating it from the public's point of view. They've determined that your activity just isn't important enough to a significant segment of their readers/viewers/listeners.

The media hate pointing out the obvious. They yearn to point out, or "uncover," the opposite of the obvious. So if the general consensus about you or your business is favorable, what good does it do any media outlet to further that story line? This is quite apparent in the way the media handle the president of the United States (whoever may occupy that position at any point in time). The president is always trying to show himself in the best light possible. So the media are always searching for some tidbit of information to the contrary. When they find something, they'll milk it for all it's worth, sometimes turning the tidbit into a mountain. Why? You know the answer: because the media want to tell people something new, and new information is almost always the opposite of the prevailing information.

For many years, Donald Trump demonstrated a masterful ability to generate favorable publicity. With every new and bigger project he undertook, his publicity grew proportionally. Unlike you and your 800-square-foot restaurant, the sheer magnitude and glitz of Trump's projects affected many people, including curiosity seekers, and therefore warranted the exposure.

But as Trump became so well-known as the squeaky clean, megarich hotel/casino magnate extraordinaire, the media became increasingly hungry for information to the contrary. Like a boulder that is pushed up a mountain side by the marketer, publicity will eventually turn in direction and come roaring down with a velocity equal to its height, often crushing the marketer in its wake. Lo and behold, in 1990, when Trump ran into difficulty with his marriage and his finances, the salivating media pounced. The media carved Trump for every ounce of dirt they could find. Only when Iraq invaded Kuwait in the summer of 1990, and the entire U.S. military went into action, did a story come along that eclipsed that of Trump.

- **People see things differently.** Why is it that two different, unbiased witnesses to the same automobile accident will tell totally conflicting accounts of what they saw? For whatever reason, people see things differently. That's why two or more different reporters can cover the same story and write completely different accounts. That's why a reporter might do a story on you (or your product, service, or business) that turns out to be completely opposite of how you or the next guy would write about you.

But what about the facts, you ask? How could a writer or reporter distort the facts so blatantly? You'd better sit down for this: The actual "facts" do not exist. The "facts" are, in reality, whatever a person believes them to be. There are no more vivid examples of this phenomenon than can be witnessed every day in the legal profession. The prosecution and the defense present completely different sets of "facts" that each seems believable. One side believes in its "facts," the other in its "facts." As it turns out, fact is based on belief, not the other way around.

- **A media outlet's angle may be opposite the marketer's angle.** Many ideas for features stories or articles come from the media people themselves, not from news events per se. So instead of waiting for something to happen and simply covering it, a reporter may decide to do a feature on "the corruption in city hall," for example, and then proceed to dig up information that supports that story line.

Let's say a reporter calls and wants to interview you. "Great," you think, "we could certainly use the publicity." You show the reporter around your restaurant and spend another hour answering questions in your office while the photographer is snapping away all along. The article comes out a few weeks later, and all that great publicity you (naively) expected is nothing of the sort. The angle of the article is the health hazards of high-cholesterol restaurant food, and there's a photo of your cook pouring cheese over eggs with a caption that reads "Patrons of restaurants like Joe's Eatery have no idea how much fat goes into their food."

Is it fair? Is it right? It's certainly debatable. Remember, the reporter's loyalty is to her employer, and the employer's (the media outlet's) loyalty is to its audience. They have no loyalty or obligation to the person they're interviewing.

The next time you read an unfavorable article about a company in *Forbes*, or watch a revealing exposé on "60 Minutes," ask yourself this: did the reporter call up and say "I'd like to interview you for a negative article I'm writing that will surely make you look like a total buffoon"? Hardly. The reporter never let on that the story might be negative (the reporter may not even have known it would end up taking on a negative slant going in). Although the marketer might object to such reporting tactics, the public—whom the media outlets serve—might be very appreciative.

So now do you think publicity should warrant more than 5 to 10 percent of your resources? Most marketers overestimate the importance of publicity. Not that great publicity isn't valuable. But it's too iffy—you can't rely on it to be there when you need it. And it's usually not of the magnitude or sustainability necessary to affect demand to any appreciable degree over the long run.

Publicity is a frill that's nice to have from time to time. In that regard, there are some things you can do to foster positive press and impede negative press. But remember, going after publicity is like stepping up to the table and rolling the dice. You may win and you may lose. Publicity seeking is not for the faint-hearted.

Here are my recommendations:

- **Don't do anything that warrants negative publicity.** If you're caught turning back odometers, you have no right to complain when the media get hold of it The higher your profile, the cleaner you need be.

- **Be honest with the media.** Of course, you needn't volunteer negative information or tell tales out of school. It's okay to put your best foot forward, or to even be a bit evasive or coy. As every politician knows, that's part of the game. Just don't tell blatant lies. A lie will always come back to haunt you, usually with great magnitude. Remember, hell hath no fury like a reporter duped.

- **Keep the press informed.** Ninety-nine percent of all "news releases" that reach an editor's desk go straight into the waste basket. But they are read. Send information to key reporters and editors on a regular basis, even though most of it generates nothing. You never know when an interest will be sparked and a story will result

- **Become a quotable "source."** Reporters quote knowledgeable people all the time (many media outlets require their reporters or writers to quote *x* number of "experts" or "authorities" per story as one measure of quality writing). Part of the material you regularly send to the media should contain quotes from you that may be lifted and used as a writer sees fit. In time, they may call you and ask for your comments regarding some aspect of the field in which you are known. One media outlet sees you quoted in another, and soon you're on numerous "source" Rolodexes. (All of this presumes you have something intelligent and worthwhile to say.)

- **Submit material for publication.** Write articles and/or submit photos. Many publications have regular columns set up to feature guest authors.

- **Avoid stunting.** Publicity stunts are nothing but cheap attempts to get media attention for no other reason than the exposure. The media hate them and try to ignore them whenever possible. Besides, you end up looking foolish most of the time, because it's obvious to everyone you're reaching when you stunt.

  Exception: If you are in the entertainment industry, or you thrive on flamboyance for whatever reason, you can successfully mount some "wild and crazy" stunt from time to time. For example, radio station disc jockeys are always doing such things as camping out on a billboard for a week, burying oneself underground for two or three days, or riding a rollercoaster for eight hours straight. Most often, though, such stunts are done in the name of fund raising for some charitable cause.

It's difficult for a media outlet to ignore or criticize a publicity seeker when the seeker is acting on behalf of a charity.

• **Let bad publicity roll off your back.** If you're a player, you're going to be tackled for a loss from time to time. Sooner or later, you'll be hit by a negative story, if for no other reason than you're visible and therefore a target. When that happens, you've got to maintain your cool and go about business as usual. Avoid retaliating, although an unemotional letter correcting any erroneous information may be appropriate. The very same media outlet that burns you one day can embrace you the next. Reporters and writers come and go, and yesterday's news is ancient history. Don't prevent yourself from getting positive press in the future by going into a tyrannical rage every time a negative story comes out.

TOOL NUMBER FOUR: CONTESTS

A contest offers the participant a chance to win something. About 10 to 20 percent of your marketing resources should be devoted to contesting.

Many marketers underestimate the value of contests. I've heard many a marketer express sentiments like these about contests:

"The public is tired of them."

"Very few people actually participate."

"A contest cheapens the image of my product."

"There's no way a small firm like ours can match the magnitude of prizes offered by the big boys, or by state lotteries."

"They require too much work for too little benefit."

"Why should I give away my product? I could go broke doing that."

Actually, all these assessments can turn out be accurate if a contest is poorly conceived or poorly executed. But for well-conceived, well-executed contests, the advantages are numerous.

The day people no longer appreciate getting something for nothing, or when they no longer enjoy having a little fun in the process, will be the day you can stop doing contests. You'll know when that day occurs, as people will suddenly stop watching "Wheel Of Fortune" and "Jeopardy," stop buying state lottery tickets, and stop visiting Vegas, Atlantic City, and the race track.

No one ever tires of getting something for nothing. Because we live in a society that constantly trades value for value, we learn "there's no such thing as a free lunch" and "nothing in the world comes free" very early in life. Anytime a person really does get something for nothing, as occurs when winning a contest, it's always a pleasurable and memorable experience.

That's exactly why the magnitude of your prizes is virtually irrelevant. Let's say you walk into a grocery store and a sounder of some kind goes off. The manager comes up to you and says "Congratulations! You're our one hundred thousandth customer! You've just won a certificate for $100 in free groceries!" Are you likely to shove the certificate back in his face, declaring in disgust, "How dare you give me only $100 worth of free groceries! I want $17 million cash like the state lottery is offering!"? There's nothing wrong with small prizes, although if the value of each prize is less than $50, a contest may become suspect.

It is true that very few people, relative to the entire population, participate in contests. But very few people, relative to the entire population, do anything. The purpose of a contest is not to elicit mass participation, anyway. It's to create excitement, to add spunk and vibrancy to your entire marketing program.

Three Types of Contests

Contests can take any one of three forms: *revolving, perennial,* and *one-shot.* The main difference is how often they're conducted.

Revolving contests are ongoing for an extended length of time (they may not have any prescheduled end). A hardware store, for example, may run a "Weekly Fix" contest and give away $75 worth of merchandise each week to a customer whose name is drawn from a barrel (one need enter only once a year). A radio or television station may run a "Free Lunch" contest in which one business or office is awarded lunch for six at a local restaurant (this is also an example of a cosponsored promotion). An apartment complex may award one month's free rent to a different tenant each month.

A perennial contest occurs each year at the same time. It is a promotional tradition. Most often perennials are built around holidays, although that is not mandatory. Miller Lite runs a Super Bowl contest every year. A radio station may run the same Christmas contest every year. Perennial contests usually build in terms of participation and payoff with each year's successive running, making them all the more valuable over time.

One-shot contests come and go, lasting only a few weeks in duration. They are not scheduled to last or repeat, although a marketer may bring back a one-shot contest some time in the future.

How to Run a Contest

Keep these points in mind regarding contests:

- **Use a combination of contest types.** Have one revolving contest in effect most of the time. Create some good promotional traditions with two or three perennials. Then leave yourself open for one or two one-shots a year. (You may not plan any specific one-shots in advance, but wait to take advantage of them as opportunities and ideas present themselves.)

- **Use a simple participation structure.** If you have trouble getting people to participate, it's probably because your contest takes too much effort to enter. Anything more than simply filling out an entry blank or guessing a simple answer is too complex.

- **Make your procedures incredibly clear.** How many contests have you not entered only because you weren't clear on what it is you were supposed to do to enter or win? If a person can't grasp the essence of your contest in the first 4 seconds, and understand how to enter and win within the first 15 seconds, it's not explained clearly enough.

- **Have lots of winners.** Many smaller-prize winners are always better than fewer larger-prize winners. If you've ever played the slot machines at Las Vegas or Atlantic City, you know they pay off in small increments all the time. The possibility of winning the big jackpot may attract you to begin with, but the small payoffs along the way keep you interested and playing for longer lengths of time.

Multiple Payoffs

Contests are a great way of attracting new customers and getting existing customers to increase their patronage. In addition, contest entry blanks are a primary vehicle for collecting names for your in-house database. Each of these benefits will be discussed further in subsequent chapters.

Chapter Three

Preparing Your Product or Service for Lift-Off

Y ou are a model rocket hobbyist. You've entered the latest competition sponsored by your club. Your goal is to build a rocket and launch it as far into the air as possible, thereby winning the contest.

You and the other contestants will be setting up your rockets in the same general area, a grassy flat of land free of obstruction. As you look around, you notice a hill about 100 feet away. The hill is a good 20 feet higher in elevation than the area in which everyone is setting up, and a thought goes through your mind. "How much higher would my rocket go," you wonder, "if I launched from the top of the hill instead of the flatland?"

Whatever height it might reach, it would be 20 feet higher if launched from the hilltop, all other factors being equal. The problem with doing so, however, is obvious. The rules of the contest prohibit one contestant from having an unfair advantage over the others, so the hilltop is off limits. You're left to rely on sheer thrust, as little wind resistance as possible, and plain old good luck to win.

But when it comes to launching the marketing rocket for your product or service, there are no rules prohibiting you—or anyone else—from launching from as high a hilltop as you can find.

No one says you have to rely strictly on the power of your engine or good luck. You can put yourself at great advantage by first climbing the hill, then launching. That way, *the same amount of marketing thrust produces a much greater result.*

YOUR PRODUCT OR SERVICE MUST BE DIFFERENT

Properly preparing your product or service before you begin marketing is the equivalent of climbing to the hilltop. And the single most important way to prepare your product or service is to create *differences* between your product or service and others available in the marketplace. The greater the differences, the higher the hill on which you stand and the greater results you'll achieve.

Marketers often make the mistake of relying on marketing alone to create the *perception* of differences, where no real differences exist. This is like launching your rocket from the bottom of a canyon. You need a whole lot of engine thrust just to get out of the hole, let alone high above ground. Even the most powerful marketing engines fail when the task is just too great. Don't place an unfair burden on your marketing program. Create *real* differences, such as those I describe below, and you'll be well ahead of the game.

THREE TYPES OF DIFFERENCES

There are three types of differences you can create: *product* or *service, packaging,* and *distribution.*

Product/Service Differences

Product/service differences are, not surprisingly, those that are inherent in your actual product or service.

In 1985, Miller Brewing Company introduced a new brand of beer called Miller Genuine Draft. To make it different from any other beer, they created a process called "cold filtering."

Pert shampoo sold poorly until Procter & Gamble created a major product difference. They made it a shampoo and conditioner in one, renaming it Pert Plus. It's now the nation's best-selling shampoo.

Motown Records was founded upon the creation of a completely different type of music, the "street sound" of Detroit. A&M Records' first product was the unusual sound of Herb Alpert & The Tijuana Brass. Casablanca pioneered disco. Island Records pioneered reggae; Delicious Vinyl, rap. If you want to launch a new record label with the best chances of success, the more different your acts sound, the better.

Each brand of cigarette must have a product difference, or it won't sell. So some are longer, shorter, or thinner; use less tar and nicotine; sell more to a pack; or have a bigger filter, no filter, menthol taste, and so on. I'm waiting for some company to launch a square cigarette. Not that square has any practical advantage over round, but it would be a major difference. Remember, the product/service differences are just that—*differences*. The differences needn't necessarily be *improvements* or *advantages*, though it's much better if they are. Ivory soap floats. A neat difference, but does that make Ivory a better soap? Who knows?

Lyle used to work as an auto sound installer at a large electronics store before starting his own auto sound business. He knew he couldn't compete with the "big boys" as a retailer, so he created a major service difference to separate himself from the competition. Lyle sold and installed sound equipment from his van at the customer's home or workplace. He came to my office and installed my system while I worked, saving me the time and trouble of having to take my car into a shop.

Packaging Differences

Packaging differences are those that affect the physical package and/or the structure of the offer. The *offer* refers to the way a product or service is grouped and priced.

Elvis Presley looked completely different from any other singer when he first appeared. So did Little Richard, The Beatles, David Bowie, and Madonna. Why do so many recording artists try to look different from the next? Because they've got to create as many packaging differences as possible between themselves and others in order to break through. By not relying strictly on the product differences of their music to do the job, they can give themselves a marketing edge.

Pringles potato chips come evenly stacked in a can. Pearl Drops tooth polish is a liquid that comes in a squeeze bottle (this is also an example of a product difference). Duracell has come up with a package that contains a built-in battery tester.

Here are a couple of examples of packaging differences that have to do with the offer. Little Caesar's gives you "two pizzas for one low price." Their two-for-the-price-of-one package uniquely positions Little Caesar's as the low-cost alternative to dine-in and delivery shops. (The fact that Little Caesar's offers only customer pick-up service, and not dine-in or delivery, is an example of a distribution difference.) When you have your film processed at Peoples Drug, you get two prints for the price of one. Goodyear sometimes offers a buy-three, get-one-free tire package.

Distribution Differences

Distribution differences are those that deal with how a product or service reaches the consumer or how it is purchased.

Domino's Pizza was founded on the home delivery principle— a major difference between Domino's and others. Yet for years many people told Domino's founder Tom Monaghan he should set up tables in his stores to capture some of the dine-in crowd as well as the eat-at-home people. Domino's could, after all, continue to deliver to those that phone-ordered, so the additional dine-in business would be that much the better, right? Perhaps, but Tom knew that if he did that, he'd suddenly appear to be just like every other pizza restaurant. The delivery feature would get lost; it would no longer be a powerful differentiator. (Domino's is looking for other ways to tap into the dine-in market without tainting their delivery-only image. They're currently experimenting with a new division called Pizzazz that sells pizza at some Burger King restaurants, and in shopping malls.)

Years ago, marketers such as Avon, Amway, and Tupperware decided the best way to compete in their respective industries was to use a different channel of distribution. So they each shunned the department stores and chose door-to-door home sales, cleverly employing Ms. Homemaker to sell to her friends and neighbors.

The Home Shopping Club took television advertising to its extreme by creating their own cable channel and producing a 24-hour-a-day, 7-day-a-week perpetual motion commercial. This distribution difference deals more with how products and services are purchased rather than how they're delivered.

MULTIPLE DIFFERENCES

Can you create all three—product/service, packaging, and distribution differences—for one product or service? Absolutely. Having one difference in each category gives you the ultimate advantage.

The classic case, used in just about every marketing class from 1974 on, is that of L'eggs Pantyhose. Prior to the introduction of L'eggs in 1970, the women's hosiery market was mature and stagnant. When the market isn't growing, you're forced to create major differences if you're to have any hope of survival, let alone major success. L'eggs did such a good job of creating differences that it became the best-selling hosiery brand in the country less than one year after introduction. Let's look at how it created various differences.

L'eggs decided from the start to create a radical product difference. Its product had to look completely different from anything else on the market. Every other brand of hose came flat, in the shape of a leg. So L'eggs did the opposite. Its product came all crumpled up in a ball—hardly what one might think of as advantageous. They turned it into an advantage, however, by playing up the product's stretchiness. "Our L'eggs fit your legs" became their slogan.

Their packaging difference was a natural extension of the product's unique look. Whereas others brands came in flat, two-dimensional cardboard packages, L'eggs came in three-dimensional plastic eggs—not only totally different, but highly recognizable in the store.

Then L'eggs added a major distribution difference. Every other major brand of hosiery was sold in department and specialty stores. So L'eggs did the opposite. It set up point-of-purchase displays called "L'eggs Boutiques" in grocery and drug stores, circumventing the department and specialty stores completely. Talk about a distribution difference! L'eggs even went one step further and set up its own fleet of trucks that pulled up *in front* of each store and delivered through the *front door* instead of the back door . . . another major difference. (L'eggs even went one step beyond that by hiring female drivers who wore the product and skin-tight "hot pants" — a sure-fire attention-getter while it lasted.)

TURN MUNDANE INTO MAGIC

Some marketers might believe it's awfully difficult to create any significant difference for the less exotic, more mundane product or service. After all, a toothbrush is a toothbrush.

Yet Johnson & Johnson altered the basic toothbrush design significantly and came up with the Reach, the first brand of toothbrush to look different in about two thousand years.

I can't think of a more mundane item than a shower head. It's nothing but a pipe end with holes. Yet Teledyne saw the opportunity to create a product difference so great it created a whole new product. The Shower Massage is a big success. Black & Decker updated the screwdriver by creating an electric version. Reebok added an air pump to a shoe and called it—what else—the Pump.

Never dismiss the opportunity to create differences, no matter how mundane your product or service. When you do a good job creating a significant difference of some kind, you can make your product or service more than a mere commodity.

CREATING YOUR DIFFERENCES

As you think of ways to make your product or service different in the three categories we discussed, keep these points in mind:

- **Strive for one difference per category.** Ideally, you have one product/service difference, one packaging difference, and one distribution difference. All three need not be monumental, though one of the three should be strong enough to dominate. More than one difference in any category can become unwieldy and can dilute the total impact of the differences.

- **More is not necessarily better.** If you can't create one difference in each category, that's okay. It's better to have one major difference, than to have multiple smaller differences in a variety of categories.

- **Don't fall into the "It's not done that way in my industry" trap.** If you determine that an idea is not feasible because it's not done that way in your industry, give it more thought before discarding it. Remember, if it's not done that way, you have a major opportunity to create a difference by doing it that way. Think of L'eggs, which broke all the "rules" and became an overnight success.

- **Don't worry about how the competition will react.** I'll tell you right now that any differences you create may not be differences for long when your competition begins copying you. Miller Lite was out for just a short time before other "light" beers appeared. (Miller Lite wasn't even the first light beer, just the first successful one.) Federal Express had the overnight package delivery business to itself for only a short time before UPS, the U.S. Postal Service, Emery, and others joined in. Domino's delivers, but now Pizza Hut has a delivery branch. L'eggs may have been the innovators extraordinaire, but it didn't take long for No nonsense to match them step for step.

Yet in each example I have just cited, the leader that originally created the differences has achieved and maintained the lion's share of the market. Let the competition do what it will; your strategy is to do what's best for you, and that's to hammer home your differences year after year, without wavering.

Chapter Four

The Six Biggest Wastes of Marketing Money

To create massive demand, you must make sure every marketing dollar you spend, especially in the advertising and promotion areas, is working for you. No marketer ever argues with that statement. Yet many well-intentioned marketers end up wasting their precious financial resources on things that are simply not destined to ever produce results.

Here are the six biggest wastes of marketing money. Avoid these budget drainers, and you'll move into the top 10 percent of all marketers in the world.

WASTE NUMBER ONE: MARKETING SHORT OF THE RESULTS THRESHOLD

In football, you score points only when you get the ball over your opponent's goal line. March the ball 99 yards downfield, but fail to get it over the goal line, and all that effort consumed by your 99-yard drive did you no good. You score the points, and receive the subsequent recognition and glory, only when you achieve that final yard and break the plane of the goal.

Marketing works the same way. You get results only when you burst through the results threshold. Stop short of the results threshold, and all the money you've spent getting 99 percent of the way there does you no good and is therefore wasted.

The $750 Ticket

Let me illustrate how this happens. Say your goal is to fly from New York to London. At Kennedy Airport, you have your choice of airliners. Jet A, fueled and ready to go, costs $1,000 a ticket. Jet B, also fueled and ready to go, costs only $750 a ticket. But there's a problem with Jet B. It has only enough fuel to fly three-quarters of the way there. Of course, you'd save $250 if you took it instead of Jet A, but you would also end up sitting on a life raft in the ocean with Jet B.

Which jet would you choose, A or B? About one out of four times I ask this question during my *Power Marketing* seminar someone in the audience decides to grab the cheap laugh bait and shouts, "Jet B! Jet B! Hawr! Hawr!" I've noticed some interesting similarities among people who go for the cheap laugh: They're always male; they always sit in the back of the room; and, from the evidence I've seen, they're always in some sort of financial trouble. The last guy who yelled "Jet B" must indeed have taken it, since his company filed for bankruptcy four months later.

Back to the action. There you are, comfortably buckled into your window seat of Jet A awaiting take-off, wondering how Hawr-Hawr is doing over there in Jet B. The jets take off, and for the first three-quarters of the way, both are flying just as high and just as fast. Which one of you looks like the smarter traveler? You in your $1,000 seat or Hawr-Hawr in his $750 dollar seat? Of course, you will arrive in London and he'll end up in the life raft, so the answer is obvious. At least it's obvious in the end. But is it obvious during the first three-quarters of the trip, when you're both traveling at the same altitude and speed?

For some people, the consequences of the $750 ticket are not obvious. They become fooled by the apparent financial "savings" at the outset and the phantom payoffs along the way. The feedback they receive from friends, family, colleagues, or competitors gives them a false perception of impact ("Hey, Fred, I saw your commercial on TV last night!"). Even when it becomes obvious that they'll never arrive, they still find solace in the illusionary "benefits" of getting three-quarters of the way there. They buy the $750 ticket again and again, spend a lot of time and money flying, but never arrive.

Examples of $750 tickets vary, depending on the industry you're in, the nature of your market, and the geographic limitations of your marketing area. For example, advertising in fringe time on a local television station or any time on a local cable system would be a $750 ticket for a national soft drink company, but might be a $1,000 ticket for a single-location mom-and-pop pizza shop that advertises home-delivered pizzas during a Friday night midnight movie.

Here's another example. A radio station decided to do a "major" direct mail contest promotion and allocated over $100,000 in prize money. Then it spent $22,000 on the direct mail piece itself, opting for a plain-looking design mailed to only about 30 percent of the households in the market. The result was a total of $122,000 spent, with virtually no measurable impact (no improvement in the ratings). Why didn't it work? The direct mail component was too watered down to burst through the results threshold.

The station should have reversed its expenditures, spending the $100,000 on a multicolor, sharp-looking direct mail piece sent to at least 70 percent of the households in the market. The $22,000 should have been allocated as prize money (given away to many winners in $100, $500, and $1,000 prizes).

Do It Big

Although it may sometimes appear otherwise with marketing, especially with advertising, there are no significant incremental payoffs along the way. The payoffs are all at the end, when you finally burst through the results threshold.

To burst through the results threshold, and create the major demand necessary to affect sales in a big way, you've got to *reach into the depths of your marketplace and impact mass numbers of people.*

What does this mean as far as your marketing program goes? It means you must *do it big.* Make major impact. Anything else is a watered-down effort, a $750 ticket to nowhere.

The Mitigation Effect

The Mitigation Effect is a natural phenomenon that lessens the impact of almost all marketing activity. It's simply an inefficiency factor—like the wires that carry electricity to your house. They have inherent resistance that eats up part of the electricity as it travels from the power plant to your house. That's why your electric company shoots out more power than you will use. If they shot out only enough to match what you're supposed to get, you'd get 95 volts coming out of your wall socket instead of 110, the difference having been eaten up by the inefficiency factor.

Because of the Mitigation Effect, your marketing activity— advertising, promotions, publicity, and contests—will suffer an impact reduction of some degree out there in the marketplace. You may think you're "blowing the market wide open" when, in fact, you're really making a minimal impact. What seems like enough going in may not be enough coming out. You must compensate for the Mitigation Effect by boosting your level of marketing activity a little above that which you think is actually enough.

WASTE NUMBER TWO: USING A WEAK OR CONFUSING MESSAGE

The second-biggest waste of marketing money occurs when your message is weak and/or confusing. Remember, your media buys cost the same whether you have a strong, cohesive message or a weak, confusing message. I know of no media outlet that offers discounts to marketers with a lousy ad or commercial. A weak or confusing message will render your media exposure ineffectual, and therefore a waste of money.

For example, a radio station once plastered their logo, which appeared as "MX-106," on billboards throughout their market. The only problem was that the station did not refer to itself as "MX-106," pronounced "Em-Ex-One-Oh-Six," on the air. It called itself "*Mix*-One-Oh-Six" on the air. Talk about a confusing message: Was "MX-106" the same station as "Mix-One-Oh-Six"? If so, why didn't its audio moniker match its visual logo? Evidently people were confused enough to avoid tuning in, as the station's ratings were so low a complete format and call letter change eventually ensued.

Prudential is running an ad campaign built around the theme that confusion sometimes exists with insurance. The problem is that the campaign actually furthers the confusion instead of clearing it up. Prudential's slogan is, "We won't let you get it until you've got it." What? The first time I heard it I thought perhaps I was at fault; I must have missed something. Then I heard NBC's Bob Costas recite the slogan on an "NFL Live!" post-game show in October 1990, after which he added, "frankly, I don't get it . . . but that's what it says here." Well, Bob, you and I aren't alone. No one gets it. The campaign or the slogan. For a slogan to be effective, it must have self-contained clarity. Prudential's is anything but.

A recent billboard and radio campaign for Aunt Sarah's Pancake House confused a lot of people. The billboard version featured a big headline that read, "Don't Eat At Aunt Sarah's." A smaller line below read, "The National Junk Food Association." I asked a few people what they thought the billboard meant. One gentleman said he thought The National Junk Food Association was some watchdog agency that found Aunt Sarah's in violation of healthy food standards. He planned to do as the board suggested: avoid eating at Aunt Sarah's. A woman said she thought Aunt Sarah's must have put the board up, but was confused as to why they don't want people to eat there. Another woman said she didn't like junk food, so she was going to avoid Aunt Sarah's. If you take the time to decipher the message, you may be able to understand what Aunt Sarah's was trying to say. But who's going to bother to do that?

Have you ever received a direct mail piece that didn't clearly indicate who the sender was, or what it was trying to sell, or what it wanted you, the recipient, to do? Just the other day I received a flyer in the mail from some marketer touting its upcoming "12 Hour Sale" with "Savings of 25 to 50 percent off our entire stock!" Although the logo was in plain sight, that didn't tell me who they were or what business they were in. I'd never heard of them before, and after reading the direct mail piece, I still don't know who they are or what they're selling.

All too often, a marketer assumes the receiver of its message (a) is paying attention, (b) cares about receiving the advertising message, (c) cares about the product advertised, and (d) has some prior knowledge of who the advertiser is and what the product is all about. Nothing could be further than the truth.

The percentage of people who know what you're all about and actually care is very small, relative to all the people in your market or trading area. To the majority of your market, your ads may very well be too weak or confusing to register.

I'm not saying you shouldn't be creative or subtle. Creativity and subtlety are useful at times. But anytime creativity or subtlety gets in the way of clarity, you're reducing the effectiveness of your message by 90 percent.

Remember, very few people are going to bother to decipher what it is you're trying to get across. Your weak or confusing ad message—even if people stop to ponder it, which is a dangerous assumption—will most likely make either no impression or the wrong impression. And to think you paid good money for that media exposure!

WASTE NUMBER THREE: MARKETING TURMOIL

The third biggest waste of marketing money occurs when you constantly change your advertising and promotional campaigns, never giving any one of them a chance to catch hold and grow. This is like constantly uprooting crops before they're ripe; you're forever sowing but never reaping.

Demand creation is a building process. Many of the techniques you'll learn to use have cumulative effects that build and intensify over time. Results don't always kick in until well after a marketing program has been underway. When you shake things up by changing too soon or too often, you're wasting your money on each successive effort, which costs money to launch but never grabs hold. This doesn't mean you should stick with a lousy ad campaign or promotion in the name of stability. Nor does it mean you should run the same ad or commercial forever. It simply means you should avoid the temptation to tamper during the critical germination period. Assuming you have a good marketing plan, stick with your plan once it's enacted.

WASTE NUMBER FOUR: MARKETING RESEARCH

As you know, marketing research can sometimes provide you with interesting and useful information. Some of it can be helpful. Most helpful research you can obtain is of three different types. The first is *secondary data,* called such because it's originally compiled by a party other than your company or a research firm you may commission. Secondary data are usually obtained from a governmental agency or trade organization. Historical information on population, economics, product sales, market share, and so on is readily available at most libraries, and the latest information can usually be found in trade publications or local and national governmental agencies for the price of a few phone calls. The second type of helpful research is *customer grading surveys.* Ask your customers or consumers to rate or grade your product or service on a number of qualities. What they say may be very illuminating. The third type of worthwhile research is *empirical observation.* Watch what people do. It's as simple as that. If there's one form of marketing research that is vastly underutilized, it's plain old observation.

But the subject of Waste Number Four is a fourth type of marketing research—the type that can not only be a waste of your money, but has the potential to destroy you. I'm talking about *perceptual* or *attitudinal* research. When you try to "get into the mind" of the public—when you attempt to identify prevalent perceptions, attitudes, interests, and opinions—you're asking for trouble. Big trouble.

Not that there aren't some very competent research professionals that can produce a well-crafted, scientifically sound research project for you. Fielding mechanics and statistical reliability are not the problem. But we humans are very funny about answering questions about ourselves. In fact, we tend to provide highly inaccurate answers to such questions, partially because we can't accurately recall things that aren't really important to us, partially because we're asked to give conscious thought and opinion to things that are primarily subconscious in nature, partially because we really want to get off the phone and the quickest way to do that is to give any random answer, partially because we really have no opinion but still feel compelled to come up with one so as not to appear uninformed or stupid, and partially because we want to give prestigious answers that make us look good.*

The bottom line: What people *say* they believe and do and what people *really* believe and do are two different things. You've seen evidence of this many times with friends, acquaintances, or family members, haven't you?

Coca-Cola discovered the trappings of marketing research the hard way in 1985. That's the year, you will recall, they did away with the time-tested, highly successful "old" Coke—the then 99-year-old formula that had built the company—and replaced it with the sweeter-tasting "new" Coke.

In April of that year, Coca-Cola Chairman Roberto Goizueta was a guest on CNN's "Moneyline" program. Host Lou Dobbs began by noting an opinion expressed by some Pepsi officials that Mr. Goizueta's decision to change the Coke formula was perhaps a foot-shooting move. To which Goizueta replied, "It's not a decision of mine. It's a decision made by the American consumers. Over 190,000 consumers have told us . . . they prefer [the new taste of Coke] over the original Coke."

---

*The "garbology" studies of the 70s illustrated this last point quite vividly. The researcher would, unbeknown to a homeowner, sift through that homeowner's trash can and find evidence of particular brand usage, empty Boone's Farm bottles, for example. Then the researcher would ring the doorbell and ask what brand of alcoholic beverage the homeowner drinks. Dom Perignon would be the answer.

"Does it ever concern you," Dobbs prodded, "about your faith in consumer research... marketing research?"

"Well," Goizueta noted, "it's so overwhelming, so absolutely overwhelming, the results we have gotten... that we revere the consumer a lot more than we revere a 99-year-old formula, to be frank with you."

You know the outcome. After mounting public outcry and declining sales, Coca-Cola admitted its blunder and revived the "old" formula, renaming it Classic Coke. They're still trying to figure out what to do with the anemic New Coke (a name change to "Coke II" is the latest rumor).

The television networks have long since been aware of the problems that can occur when you actually believe—and act upon—your marketing research. In research survey after research survey, "documentaries" would be the type of television program that most people say they prefer. So the networks would produce documentaries. And sure enough, they would end up as the least-watched shows time and time again. Research also indicates that most people object to shows with "too much sex and violence." Yet those shows usually end up at the top of the ratings. That's why you don't see many documentaries anymore. And that's why the majority of the characters on television today are either involved in slimy and tawdry sexual escapades week after week or they carry a gun and shoot at people.

Why Do It?

If marketing research is so unreliable, why do so many companies spend so much time and money doing so much of it? Here's why:

- **Debate reduction.** When you have a menagerie of decision makers, debates can rage on and on. (Helen Slater to Michael J. Fox in *The Secret of My Success:* "There is no right or wrong, there is only opinion.") Research can be the arbiter that no one in the organization is willing to be.

- **Decision justification.** In a highly charged political environment, research may be your best ally. Heaven forbid you should put your own judgment on the line by making a decision or mounting a cause without plenty of research to back you up. When the finger of guilt inevitably points your way one day, you can in turn point to the research, shrug your shoulders, and emerge virtually unscathed. Roberto Goizueta is still the chairman of Coca-Cola.

- **Anxiety reduction.** Decisions can sometimes be tough to make. But when you've got a two-inch-thick research report pointing the way, it somehow becomes easier.

- **Competition matching.** All of your competitors do it, so it must be worthwhile, right? Besides, you can't bear the thought that a competitor might just happen to stumble onto something, leaving you without so much as a line in the water.

- **It's addictive.** Research addicts feel they must have it monthly, weekly, daily, with every breath.

How Do You Kick the Habit?

- **Admit you don't need it.** The next time you're thinking of commissioning another project, think first about the five reasons for research I named above. Then ask yourself this question: If a situation demands debate reduction, decision justification, anxiety reduction, competition matching, or an addictive fix, doesn't the company or individual(s) in question have far greater problems than research could ever treat? Realize that the answer to any problems or opportunities that lie before you will not be found through marketing research— no more than water can be found with a divining rod.

- **Be skeptical of research findings.** The worst thing you can do is spend lots of money on perceptual or attitudinal research and then actually believe and act upon the findings. When you allow research to overrule your instincts and common sense, you're allowing bytemites (obsessive computer number crunchers) to run your life.

A research project from time to time won't hurt you as long as you learn to treat the findings with less than a grain of salt. The television networks spend millions on research each year yet have learned to ignore the majority of it. In radio, research reveals that the thing listeners complain about most is disc jockeys "talking over the music." So what do the disc jockeys do at the most successful, highest-rated stations? Talk over the music. (Talking over the music creates excitement and stimulates emotions, which is desired by the subconscious. But listeners don't consciously know this; they don't know their brain actually likes the result of disc jockeys' talking over the music.)

Absolut vodka is the largest-selling imported vodka in the United States. According to *Forbes*, Absolut spent $65,000 in 1978 on a major research project that concluded Absolut would fail in the United States because, among other things, the bottle didn't have a paper label and the neck was too small for bartenders to grab. How did Absolut's president, Michel Roux, react? He threw the research out, noting "I just felt they didn't know what they were talking about."

- **Save your money.** Once you learn to ignore research findings, the obvious question becomes, "Why spend money on it in the first place?" Save your money for the action-oriented tasks you'll be engaged in later.

WASTE NUMBER FIVE: CORE OVERKILL

Almost every marketer has a primary marketing target for each product or service. It's usually expressed in standard demographic terms, such as males aged 25 to 44 for audio/video equipment or females aged 18 to 39 for a particular line of bedroom furniture.

Many marketers also like to compress their primary target into as thin or precise a demographic slice (demo) as possible—compressing the male 25–44 demo down to males 25–34 with yearly incomes in the $28,000–$55,000 range who own their own homes, for instance. A thinly defined demographic target is called a *core*. The more compressed or thin your core, the easier it is to cater to the common needs of core people. From a media-buying standpoint, it's also easier and cheaper to reach the core versus a much wider demo slice.

Core marketing, or "niche" marketing as it's sometimes called, has its advantages at times. But here's the rub: As a marketer continues to concentrate on a core over time, an ever-increasing percentage of the core-targeted marketing becomes ineffectual. In other words, your core becomes saturated when core people are not going to buy any more of your product than they are already buying, no matter how many more marketing missiles you bombard them with. Therefore, once you've maximized your core, a large percentage of your subsequent core-targeted marketing is useless, a waste of money. You've reached the point of diminishing returns as far as your core is concerned.

Because so many marketers make the recurring mistake of allocating too much of their marketing budget to core-targeted activity, and because doing the opposite—targeting to a much wider slice of the market—can be extremely advantageous at times, I have devoted all of Chapter 11 to its further discussion.

WASTE NUMBER SIX: LARGE PRIZE CONTESTS WITHOUT MASS MARKET EXPOSURE

As I mentioned in Chapter 2, you don't need large, big-ticket prizes to run an effective contest. (Let's define large as anything over $1,000 in value.) That doesn't mean large prizes are superfluous, however. They can be useful in attracting new consumers or customers who otherwise wouldn't make the effort to enter your contest and buy your product or service.

To make your large prizes pay off—that is, to use them as bait to attract many new customers—you need mass market exposure of your contest. You need to reach those people who are not presently buying your product. If, on the other hand, you do not arrange for mass market exposure of your contest, instead reaching mainly your existing customers through an entry blank attached to the product or an in-store display, save your money and go with much smaller prizes. Your existing customers simply do not need large prizes to motivate them to enter the contest or buy more from you. For them, smaller prizes are just as effective.

Here's the rule: Fuel a mass-marketed contest with large prizes, and fuel a non–mass-marketed contest with small prizes.

PART 2

THE PSYCHOLOGY OF DEMAND

The term *demand* connotes a common desire among many people for a particular product or service. A handful of people who want a product does not constitute demand. To create demand, you must reach and affect a whole lot of people—thousands, tens of thousands, or millions.

But before you are ready to reach out to the masses, you must reduce demand down to its simplest form and understand how it works, as scientists might examine a single human cell to determine how to act on the whole human body more effectively.

People don't gather together as one multiperson unit and collectively decide whether or not to purchase your product or service. That decision is made on an individual basis, one human brain at a time. In this section, we'll discuss the psychology of demand—what goes on inside the mind of the individual. You'll learn how to create *want* and *desire* in the minds of individuals, the first step in demand creation.

Chapter Five

What People
Really Want

P eople want a lot of things: love, success, fun, health, secu-
rity, companionship, money, you name it. Man is, indeed,
a "wanting animal," and the true boundaries of man's want are
limitless.

You needn't be concerned with the enormity of man's want,
however. As a marketer, you can gain tremendous advantage
simply by understanding the top four things people really want
to attain when they purchase any product or service. Once you
learn what those four wants are, you can mold your marketing accordingly. This is the beginning of the demand-building process.

The top four wants, either individually or in some combination, provide the powerful motivation behind the purchase of
virtually any and all products or services. We call them the *power-
wants*. They are inherent in all people, regardless of sex, race, age,
nationality, social background, or economic status. The power-
wants are strong and potent. As we discuss each, think of ways
you can use them in your own marketing program.

Note: Beginning now, and continuing throughout the book, I'll
be using some specific, real-life ad campaigns as examples. Most

are from large, nationally known marketers. I use large-scale marketers as examples because that is what you are most likely to be familiar with. Please don't infer that the techniques under discussion are only for large-scale marketers. They're for you, regardless of the scale you're operating on.

POWER-WANT NUMBER ONE: EMOTIONAL STIMULATION

Most of the time our emotions lie dormant, waiting in anxious anticipation for any spark that will trigger their release. And when human emotions flow, the result is a psychologically pleasing experience. We humans crave emotional stimulation.

Mostly, people desire positive emotional feelings such as love, excitement, laughter, and sexual attraction. But the desire for emotional stimulation is so strong that people even enjoy feeling negative emotions at times. In a strange way, such negative emotions as fear, sadness, loneliness, and anger can be enjoyable. That's why you see lines of people waiting to see a horror movie or ride a "death-defying" roller coaster. That's why they like sad songs and tear-jerking movies. Has your spouse or boyfriend/girlfriend ever started an argument just for the sake of arguing? Sometimes even negative emotion is better than no emotion.

Think about how emotional stimulation relates to product purchases. Why do people purchase recorded music? The superficial reason is that they like a particular song or recording artist. The real reason is that certain music stimulates their emotions.

Why do people attend sporting events? To see their favorite team or player in action? Once again, the real underlying reason is that the whole event can be an emotionally stimulating experience.

Why do children love to get toys for Christmas and hate getting clothes? What do the toys do that the clothes do not?

Why do you take snapshots or video tape an event? Could it be because the photos or tape are great triggers that cause you to re-experience the emotion of the event again and again?

Provide Emotional Stimulation in Your Advertising

Okay, people want their emotions stimulated. So how does that happen? How do you, the marketer, provide emotional stimulation? Most often, your product or service itself won't be able to stimulate an emotion nearly as well as your *advertising* of the product or service. Put another way, your advertising, not your product or service, contains the emotion-stimulating force in most cases.

Take fast food, for example. A hamburger, fries, and soft drink are not emotional things. Even consuming them isn't an emotional experience. Yet McDonald's advertisements show people in highly emotional states—high-school kids gathering to flirt with the opposite sex; mom, dad, and the kids coming to McDonald's as a family event; or McDonald's employees smiling, laughing, and dancing. The ads stimulate an emotion, to which the product is linked.

Build Psychological Links

The idea is to create *psychological links* between your product and a strong emotion. In your advertising, you first create an emotional situation, then link your product or service with it. The concept is really quite simple.

Look how Coke and Pepsi do it. In a recent television commercial for Coke, you see the New Kids On The Block in concert. They are creating excitement and joy. Then you see them holding up cans of Coke. The product has been linked.

One of Pepsi's commercials shows Michael J. Fox meeting his new female neighbor, to whom he is immediately attracted. The sexual attraction emotion has just been created. She asks for a Pepsi, and he scrambles to get her one. The product has been linked.

How to Provide Emotional Stimulation
in Your Advertising

Exactly how do you create an emotional situation and link your product/service to it in your advertising? Follow this three-step approach:

- **Step 1: Select the emotion you wish to stimulate.** The four strongest positive emotions in advertising are *excitement, love, sexual attraction,* and *laughter.*

  Some negative emotions are just as strong as these four positive emotions but are a lot trickier to use effectively. That's because people aren't always going to be paying close attention to your advertising, and they can inadvertently link your product with the negative emotion in their mind, even though you didn't intend for that to happen. What might happen if your ad or commercial were to depict a person angry with himself for not purchasing your product or service? The casual receiver of that ad or commercial might inadvertently link the negative emotion—anger—with your product or service in his mind.

  Let's discuss each of the four main positive emotions and see which might be best for you.

  The excitement emotion means the same thing as joy or fun. Think about the ways your ad or commercial can elicit feelings of joy or fun. Pontiac, for example, shows scenes of the car moving down water-slicked roadway, with music pumping and people interacting in the nighttime. The action is fast-paced and intense. The tag line, "We build excitement. Pontiac," spoon-feeds it to you. Excitement is established, and Pontiac is linked.

  Cigarette marketers like to link their products to excitement. They show active people in a high state of excitement, surfing or playing volleyball on the beach, racing automobiles, or rounding up cattle. Actually, these activities, as exciting as they may be, inherently have nothing to do with smoking—but so what? No rule says linkage has to make logical sense.

  Creating the love emotion is usually done by depicting interaction between family members. Because most people have strong feelings of love for members of their own family, it's easy to interpret. Hallmark, Kodak, McDonald's, and Coca-Cola have used family scenes in their advertising for years.

Perhaps the best recent use of the love emotion is Michelin's. It attached an emotionally neutral object—a tire—to a love-packed object—a baby. What two items could be more opposite in creating the love emotion than a tire and a baby? Nevertheless, the Michelin campaign linked the two. In fact, to enhance the link and make the bond between the baby and Michelin as strong as possible, it shows nothing but a baby crawling around a tire. That's it. Baby and tire. Simple and powerful. The slogan hammers it home: "Because So Much Is Riding On Your Tires." In other words, if you love your children, you'll buy Michelin tires. Buy another brand, and your children must not be important to you.

Sexual attraction is one of the most commonly used emotions in advertising because it's relatively easy to depict. The above-mentioned Pepsi commercial with Michael J. Fox uses sexual attraction, as does the McDonald's ad with the flirting teens. Michelob's "The Night Belongs to Michelob" campaign shows members of the opposite sex interacting in nightclub settings. Calvin Klein depicts sexual attractiveness in its clothing ads, as do Levi's and Guess. Hanes's "Gentlemen Prefer Hanes" campaign shows men ogling women wearing the product.

Laughter is stimulated through humor. The one drawback to humor is that oftentimes the joke upstages the product. Energizer's commercial-crashing bunny is funny, but it turns out that a lot of people don't realize the commercial is for Energizer batteries. Many people who do realize it's a battery commercial mistake it for Duracell (which used toy characters in its advertising before Energizer used the bunny). The best way of preventing the joke from overshadowing your product is to make the name of your product the punch line. Kellogg's Nut 'N Honey cereal does just that, as the brand name is played upon ("nothin' honey") in a series of humorous vignettes.

- **Step 2: Depict one or more people experiencing the emotion you are stimulating.** You establish an emotion, and cause your audience to feel it, by showing people experiencing the emotion. Show the emotion in their faces and in their voices.

Note: You don't necessarily need visual images to provide emotional stimulation. You can depict emotion in voices and in written copy as well.

- **Step 3: Depict the purchase of, or the use of, your product or service.** After establishing the emotion, show people using your product. Or do it the other way around by showing people using your product, then experiencing the emotion as a result. Or show people experiencing the emotion while simultaneously using your product (the audience will often assume a cause-and-effect relationship even if you don't spell it out).

Honing Your Emotion-Creating Skills

Creating emotion-stimulating advertising is not always easy. It's more art than science, and it takes a good deal of practice and experience to become good at it. You needn't become good at it, though. You can, and should, commission good, talented people to do it all for you, people who do this sort of thing for a living. They can be found at advertising agencies and art/commercial production firms. As for you, simply understanding the importance of emotion in your advertising is sufficient.

If, however, you're in the creative end of advertising or commercial production, or you choose to be integrally involved in your own ad creation, you may want to hone your skills accordingly. If you want to become good at creating advertising that stimulates emotions, follow the advice of one industry artist.

James Gartner, of the Los Angeles firm Gibson/Lefebvre/Gartner, directs television commercials. (Although a number of people are involved in the creation of a television commercial, it is the director who actually does what we've just talked about—create the emotion and link the product.) Gartner has directed commercials for AT&T, IBM, Federal Express, and Kodak, to name a few. His trademark is emotion-stimulating—sometimes heartwrenching—commercials.

"Surround yourself with good art, literature, film," he suggests. "Then dissect it. What is it about that particular piece that makes it stand out? In the case of a television commercial, play it back on your VCR 50 times. Notice the framing of each scene. The cutting. The pacing. The facial expressions. The dialogue. The lighting. The colors. Every element is important. It's the synergy of how those elements are used. Pay attention to details. The smallest detail is often the difference between good and great. Nothing communicates better than emotion in advertising."

POWER-WANT NUMBER TWO: PSYCHOLOGICAL RELIEF

We all have situations that produce feelings of psychological discomfort. Certain responsibilities and pressures can result in feelings of anxiety and stress. Our minds instinctively and subconsciously seek ways to relieve these feelings. If your product helps reduce or relieve psychological discomfort, people will want it.

Say you have the worst lawn in the neighborhood. You don't have time to till the ground, plant grass seed, spread fertilizer, and nurture the lawn. But the pressures to "do something" about the problem are mounting. You feel the anxiety and frustration increasing as time goes on. Finally, when the psychological discomfort is great enough, you take action to relieve it. You decide to call a professional lawn service. Once you hire it, the pressure—and psychological discomfort—is relieved.

How to Provide Psychological Relief

Providing psychological relief in your advertising works the same way as providing emotional stimulation. You depict relief and link your product or service. If the link is clear and strong, your product is perceived as a *provider* or *facilitator* of the relief.

There are the three steps in linking your product or service with psychological relief.

- **Step 1: Choose the particular psychological discomfort you want to relieve.** Anxiety, frustration, disappointment, sadness, fright, desperation, anger, loneliness, and despair are a few possibilities. What type of discomfort would your consumers or customers most likely experience if they didn't use your product or service?

• **Step 2: Depict your product or service providing psychological relief.** There are two ways of doing this. One way is to establish the discomfort first, then introduce your product or service as the reliever. Napa Auto Parts shows a vehicle stuck on a railroad track with a train barreling down. Fright and despair. You *feel* frightened just looking at the scene, don't you? Luckily, the vehicle had Napa parts. It starts at the last second and the driver pulls away unharmed. Discomfort, product, relief. In that order.

The other way is simply to establish the relief without ever establishing the prior discomfort. You imply a particular discomfort existed or would have existed prior to the product's use. Domino's Pizza, for example, shows a person picking up the phone and ordering a pizza (or, in radio commercials, it uses the sound of touch tones). As that occurs, the caller is depicted in a very happy state, as he is now relieved of having to worry about preparing dinner. Anxiety and hunger are the implied discomforts.

• **Step 3: Assume responsibility.** When you assume some responsibility for results, you're reassuring people that they will be relieved by no longer having to worry about the problem. Isn't this what the person is really buying anyway?

Federal Express points out their competence in getting your valuable package to its destination overnight. The "Absolutely, Positively Overnight" campaign said that when you use Federal Express, you no longer have to worry about your valuable package. The "Why Fool Around with Anyone Else?" campaign actually implied you'd better worry if you use another overnight service.

Orkin gives you a written guarantee of their responsibility, and tells you so in their advertising. If a pest reappears within a specified length of time after treatment, they'll come back and fix the problem at no charge. That's assuming responsibility.

Midas will replace your new muffler free for as long as you own the car. Buy from Midas, and you no longer have to worry about your muffler. That's assuming responsibility. Craftsman tools are guaranteed for life. When you own one, you no longer have to worry about it breaking. If it does, Sears replaces it free. That's assuming responsibility.

If you don't like your Florsheim Comfort Tech shoes within 30 days of purchasing them, you can return them and get your money back. That type of guarantee is unheard of in the shoe business. That's really assuming responsibility.

Link Relief to the Purchase Decision

You may have noticed that in many cases you can depict psychological relief as occurring *at the time of the purchase decision* rather than when the product or service is actually used. Domino's shows a person experiencing relief when ordering the pizza, not necessarily having to wait until eating the pizza to experience relief. When you hired the lawn care company, didn't you feel relieved right after making the call? You don't have to wait until they begin or even complete the job to feel the relief, do you?

In consulting, it's quite common for clients to feel major psychological relief as soon as they hire the consultant, well before any work is actually done. Some consultancies, including my own firm, will sometimes emphasize the immediacy of relief following the hiring decision. We do this in our advertisements and in our sales material, using precisely worded copy, with no pictures at all.

When you depict psychological relief at the time of the purchase decision, you strengthen the link between relief and your product or service and thus increase your impact appreciably.

POWER-WANT NUMBER THREE: HIGHER STATUS

From the beginning of mankind, every human society has "ranked" its members by some stated or implied class structure. From hunting and gathering times to the feudal days of serf and king to modern times, every society has been organized by some type of social class strata. (Animals operate the same way, too.) Social scientists have long been interested in the phenomenon, and the number of studies that have been done on the subject could fill the room you're sitting in now.

But all you need to know about it is this: People seek to gain higher social status. The tendency to want higher status is instinctive and normal, and is averted only when a person consciously chooses otherwise. (Even some religious orders that denounce money and other material possessions as measures of social stature are still subject to their own internal pecking order based on whatever measures they've chosen.)

Some people are, of course, more status-conscious than others, but only to an insignificant degree. What often appear to be differences in status consciousness are actually differences in status *circles*, not consciousness. In other words, your neighbor may not wear Armani suits or drive a Mercedes, but that doesn't mean he's oblivious to status. It just means he's not in the same circle as those who use Armani and Mercedes to display status. Perhaps an Orvis fishing pole and Chevrolet pickup truck are considered status symbols in his circle. All people seek higher status; they just display it in different ways, according to the "rules" of their particular circle.

Do you know of anyone who demonstrates an obvious disdain for status in one way or another? I know a multimillionaire who dresses like a bum and another who drives a broken-down 1977 Plymouth. Some people feel compelled to display their irreverence for status altogether. Why? Because to them, antistatus is status. In their circle, they gain in status when they display irreverence for it. (Of course, they usually make up for it in other ways. Both the people cited above live in elaborately furnished mansions.)

Higher status, or prestige, is not limited to the overall class structure dictated by wealth. There are an infinite number of smaller strata structures that exist in all segments of society, from the workplace to the social organization, from the school to the home. Each has its own set of "rules" that dictate status.

For example, our children learn about social classes and pecking orders very young. The Boy Scouts and Girl Scouts have a formal ranking structure that teaches the relative value of each rank and rewards hard work with raises in rank. Even renegade street gangs have status structures. Many so-called "gang wars" are over nothing more than status supremacy. In high school we learn quickly that sophomores are peons, juniors are respectable, and seniors are almighty. I can still remember when sophomore year was finally over; I felt as though I'd been instantly pulled out of the depths of desolation and anointed with honor. Now the new crop of lowly sophomores can wallow in the quagmire and adulate us exalted juniors! Status can be most exhilarating.

How People Attain Higher Status

The way people gain higher status is to *associate* themselves with things that provide higher status and *disassociate* with things that provide lower status.

For example, people buy and wear designer clothes because of the status association. A designer label on your clothes is like a sign on your back that says "I'm in [this particular] class."

Automobiles are strong status symbols. Remember when every 30-year-old yuppie in the 80s felt compelled to drive a BMW or Mercedes? He had to show others in his circle that he'd "made it."

Even relatively inexpensive automobiles can be status symbols. Remember, just because a person drives a Honda Accord doesn't mean she's unconcerned about status. It just means that within her circle the Accord provides some degree of status.

Why do people naturally gravitate toward celebrities? For whatever reason, celebrities are, in general, perceived to be of high status. When people ask for an autograph or to have their picture taken with a celebrity, they're really trying to gain higher status for themselves by the association.

Speaking of celebrities, they too crave higher status. Performers in concert hate being the first on the bill, since "opening" is low status. "Headlining," playing last on the bill, is high status. If someone had set it up just the opposite, and higher status had been associated with playing first, performers would want to open.

In sports, it is the opposite, where playing first is status. Think about how many professional athletes strive to be a "starter" (starting quarterback, starting pitcher, or simply in the starting lineup). Somewhere along the line, prestige became associated with starting, so athletes aspire to start.

By the way, if a coach wants to keep his nonstarting players happy in their backup roles, all he has to do is change some status associations. For example, a football coach could begin by throwing out the terms "first string" and "second string." The starting quarterback could still be called the starter, but the other quarterbacks would be called "ace relievers," as in baseball. Second, he could portray the reliever as cool and capable, not as a green schoolboy who's finally given a chance or an over-the-hill ex-starter who has to prove he's "still got it." Third, the coach should put the reliever(s) into the game from time to time, not once in a blue moon; this shows that it's not shameful for a starter to be replaced. Since replacing the starter with a reliever would occur quite often, it would be considered standard procedure, not something that indicates failure.

All it would take is for one professional football team to pay a relief quarterback as much as it pays the starting quarterback, and the prestige associated with the relief position (on all teams) would be forever cast. Isn't this what happened in baseball? Since the advent of baseball, a relief pitcher was considered inferior to a starting pitcher. Until 1984. That's the year the Atlanta Braves signed "ace reliever" Bruce Sutter to a six-year, $9.6 million contract—making Sutter the highest-paid pitcher in baseball at the time. Since then, it's been just as prestigious to be a reliever as it is to be a starter in baseball.

People also disassociate with people and things they perceive as low status. In every school, there are always one or two kids that no other kids will have anything to do with. These outcasts may understandably, though mistakenly, conclude that no one likes them, or that there's something wrong with them. But that has nothing to do with it. The reason they lack peer acceptance is that they're perceived as low status, and others feel compelled to disassociate. Every once in a while an outcast will do something that causes others to embrace him. Did the outcast suddenly change his personality or become another person? No. He just changed his status.

Products and services have perceived levels of status, which can vary depending on social circles. Why is it that many people have no trouble buying certain items of clothing at Kmart, yet these same people would die before admitting that's where their clothes came from? Some people perceive Kmart as so low in status that they wouldn't set foot in the store if Kmart were giving away the merchandise. (Kmart shouldn't be singled out in this regard; Wal-Mart, Ames, or any other discount retailer represents the same degree of low status to some.) To its credit, Kmart has been trying to raise its status level in recent years. That's one reason it hired Jaclyn Smith and put her name on a line of clothing. And why it's refurbishing its stores to attain a more contemporary look.

Watch what people say and do with regard to disassociation. When someone expresses a dislike for a particular product or service, it can quite often be traced directly back to a desire to disassociate based on a lack of perceived status. Although she says otherwise, a person's dislike may not have anything to do with the actual product qualities; no one likes to consciously admit that status is the underlying factor.

How to Provide Higher Status

When you link your product or service to something or someone that represents a certain level of status, some of that status will transfer or rub off onto your product or service.

There are a number of ways to link your product or service with some level of status, but here are the three most potent:

- **Price.** In a capitalist society, money is the single most significant measure of status. People purchase things that have high prices because display of such items shows that the buyer has money.

  Cuisinart food processors sell for considerably more than food processors made by Waring or Oster. Cuisinart made an interesting observation years ago. People don't put their food processors away, out of sight, when they're not using them. They keep them sitting on the kitchen counter. Anytime you have a product or service that the buyer "displays" in full view of others, you have an opportunity to use status to your advantage. By charging a comparatively high price for its product, Cuisinart made its food processor a major status symbol.

  Clothes marketers have discovered that a designer label alone doesn't result in great demand. However, by charging three times as much for a designer label garment as other comparable non–designer label garments, instant status erupts—and so do sales.

  Rolex sells an awful lot of high-priced watches. If you can afford a Rolex, you must be important.

  The same goes for Waterford crystal, Jenn-Air ranges, Montblanc pens, and Gucci shoes.

  Obviously, a high price strategy is not for every marketer. Many marketers do very well with a low price strategy. But watch out. Contrary to outward appearances, competing on the basis of price alone is a tough, tough game to play. The toughest kid in the neighborhood eventually runs across someone a little bit tougher. There's always another marketer somewhere willing or able to cut her price below yours. When you play the low price game, your playground is laden with quicksand. Vulnerability reigns, and you spend so much time looking over your shoulder you can lose sight of where you're going.

  But you say your product or service is so common you can't realistically raise the price and still be competitive? That may be true if your product is a commodity item, where there are few perceived differences among brands. Then again, if you've created some significant product/service, packaging, or distribution differences, you may pull your product out of the commodity hole. After all, there's nothing more common in the world than water. Most of it doesn't even have a brand name. Yet Perrier and Evian bottle it and sell it for around 30 times more than what it costs you for the same amount of tap water from the kitchen sink.

The owner of a small accounting firm was making a mediocre living until he gathered the courage to raise his prices to three times their previous level. When questioned about price, he'd say, "You hire $50-an-hour accountants, you get $50-an-hour advice. You hire $150-an-hour accountants, you get $150-an-hour advice." His business has been booming ever since.

Isn't that ripping people off? Paying more for something doesn't seem like much of a benefit to the consumer, does it? It isn't if they get a second-rate product or service. But if you're the best, you deserve to charge for it. And the consumer benefits by getting the best in return. I cited Federal Express, Craftsman tools, L'eggs pantyhose, and Domino's Pizza in earlier examples. It shouldn't surprise you that each of these marketers charges relatively high prices in their respective product categories. People have no problem paying top dollar when they get top quality in return. That's another reason why a higher price can result in higher demand.

- **Celebrity endorsements.** Celebrities represent status. That's why you see so many products and services endorsed by celebrities. A celebrity can give a product or service instant status.

Celebrities must have quite an allure to command the endorsement fees they do. Pepsi paid Michael Jackson $15 million to appear in two Pepsi commercials (he didn't even hold up a can). Pepsi paid Madonna $5 million to appear in one commercial (it ran on network television only once).

The "sneaker wars" are interesting. Nike's got Bo Jackson and Michael Jordan. L.A. Gear has Joe Montana and Michael

Jackson. Reebok used to have Paula Abdul; now L.A. Gear has her. Each celebrity earns well into the millions for each endorsement.

Can't afford a Jackson, Montana, or Abdul? Try hiring local celebrities in whatever market(s) you trade in. Nutri-System hires local radio personalities all over the country. Or create a celebrity. Car dealers have been doing it for years. I'll bet there's at least one car dealer in your home town who's as well-known as the mayor.

• **Status depiction.** Simply depict people (unknowns) in a relatively high-status situation using your product or service.

Grey Poupon does it by showing affluent people going out of their way to ask for the mustard. Johnnie Walker Black Label shows two neighbors standing outside their mansions discussing the product. Tasters Choice coffee shows a classy woman borrowing the product from a neighbor who informs her that "Tasters Choice is a very sophisticated coffee."

As I've pointed out before, status is relative. The way you depict status in your advertising depends on the way status is determined in the circle(s) you're targeting. In some circles, driving an Oldsmobile is high status; in other circles it's low status. In some circles, drinking Budweiser is high status; in other circles not.

Incidentally, it's usually advantageous to depict status at one or two levels higher than that of your target consumer. People want higher status; they want to associate with things that pull them up a notch or two. For example, Boone's wine shows middle class people using the product. Yet the lower class, not the middle class, buys it. The middle class is buying Gallo, which depicts the upper middle class in its advertising.

Want to appeal to teens? Never say your product or service is for "teens." If they perceive it to be targeted to "teens," they will disassociate. Instead, say it's for adults, and show people aged 18–24 using it. Teens want adult status and will instantly latch onto things that offer it.

POWER-WANT NUMBER FOUR: WHAT OTHERS WANT

People want what other people want. In other words, the value you and I place on things is largely influenced by the value other people place on those things.

The only way children learn to value things is through what they're taught by their parents, teachers, and peers (and, of course, the television set). How else does a child learn that a quarter is worth more than a dime? How does a child learn the value of anything? From others, of course.

Adults are affected the same way. We're constantly influenced by our employer, spouse, co-workers—anyone we come in contact with. And by advertising. On a daily basis, we are influenced by our awareness of what others value, although that awareness may be largely subconscious.

Here's an illustration of what I'm talking about. Say a big-time boxing match is scheduled to take place in your city. People all over the country are converging on your hometown—reporters, fans, the works. The excitement level gets higher as the event gets closer. Everyone you come in contact with is talking about the event and clamoring to get tickets. Most of your relatives and friends don't have tickets but wish they could somehow get hold of one or two. Suddenly, an old friend pops out of the shadows and offers you a pair. He'll sell you two tickets at the printed price, the only stipulation being that you don't resell them. Would you buy the tickets?

If you're like most people, you'd jump at the opportunity. You've seen evidence as to how valuable those tickets are, and you're not about to let them slip through your hands. Even if you had no previous interest in boxing, you want the tickets, and you're going to attend. Very few people would avoid getting so caught up in the excitement as to refuse the tickets.

Now let's look at the same situation with only one slight difference: same two fighters, same high stakes, same venue, same day and time, but no reporters and no crowds of people swarming the city. No one you know even mentions the event. Plenty of tickets are available, and your shadowy friend calls with his two-ticket offer. Would you buy the tickets? Evidently no one else wants the tickets, so why should you? If you're like most people, you would pass on the tickets this time.

Look what happens with the stock market. When stocks are rising, and value is increasing, more and more people become interested in buying. If other people want it, we want it. Conversely, when stocks are dropping, people want to bail out. If others don't want the stock, neither do we.

Here's an experiment you can try sometime. Ask someone to evaluate a party he recently attended. A simple "How was the such-and-such party?" is all you need to ask. Ninety-five percent of the time, the person answering will base his opinion strictly on the number of people that showed up. If the place was jammed, the party was "great!" If few people attended, the party "stunk." If the answerer bases his evaluation on anything other than the number of people who attended, you can bet it was his party. You see, people value a party based on how many other people valued it enough to attend.

How to Link Your Product or Service with Want

The idea is to portray your product or service as wanted by many people. You can do that by implying an existing state of demand. Here are some examples.

The owner of a new restaurant asked his employees to park their cars in front, as close to the door as possible, so that people driving by got the impression it was busy.

My dentist told me how he linked himself with want when he first began his practice years ago. He instructed his receptionist to schedule appointments overlapping each other on the same day so that patients would see one another coming and going. Even though he only had a few patients at first, it appeared he was busy.

Six months after Subway Sandwiches opened in 1965, it was in financial trouble, close to ruin. What did it do? Why, expanded, of course. Subway opened a second store and promoted it with flyers thanking everyone for making the first one "so successful." Soon the illusion of demand produced real demand.

An attorney I know instructed his receptionist to always say he was either "in court" or "meeting with a client" whenever anyone called. This guy must really be good because he's evidently very busy helping a lot of people, right? Actually, he *was* busy giving his dart board a good workout half the time. But what would people think if he actually came to the phone right when they called? They'd get the impression he wasn't in demand, hardly the type of attorney anyone would want to hire.

SUMMARY

What people *really* want, and expect to attain by purchasing something, is seldom obvious. As you may have noticed, the power-wants—the motivating forces behind all purchase decisions—are deeply subconscious. Even we, as consumers, are seldom aware of what we really want. As a matter of fact, people won't admit they want certain things even after they become aware that they do!

Remember, the idea is to psychologically link your product or service with one or more of the power-wants: emotional stimulation, psychological relief, higher status, and what others want. The stronger the link, the more people will want your product or service.

POWER-WANT CHECKLIST

Each time you prepare an ad or commercial, a promotion or contest, run it through the following series of questions. You may not be able to use all of the power-wants all of the time, but this checklist will keep you from inadvertently forgetting one that may make the difference between minor and major results.

1. Are you stimulating an emotion in your photos, speech, or written copy? What emotion(s) are you stimulating?

2. Are you offering psychological relief? What discomfort(s) are you relieving? Are you taking some responsibility so the buyer can feel he no longer has to worry about the situation once he purchases your product or service?

3. Is your product or service connoting a particular level of status? Is the level of status you connote at least one level higher than that of your target consumer?

4. Are you implying an existing, strong degree of demand? Are you letting people know that many others value your product or service highly?

Chapter Six

Magnetizing Your Marketing

Whenever I ask people to name a few qualities or attributes of good marketing, I get answers like these: creative, memorable, penetrating, clever, different, grabbing, and persuasive. I'm sure you can add one or two more to the list.

Next question: If you want your marketing to have some of these desirable qualities, how do you go about getting them? In other words, just what makes your marketing penetrating, memorable, or persuasive? Do you know exactly how to get these qualities, or do you just do your best and hope they somehow appear?

There are four main factors that determine the effectiveness of any marketing program. I call them the *power-attractors*. When you make good use of one or more of the power-attractors, your marketing will be penetrating, memorable, persuasive, and more. By proper application of the power-attractors, you will magnetize your marketing, greatly enhancing your product's attractiveness.

DIFFERENCES FROM POWER-WANTS

There are three important differences between the power-attractors and the power-wants we discussed in the previous chapter. First, unlike the power-wants, which are deeply imbedded in the subconscious, the power-attractors are much closer to the surface. People are usually consciously aware of the power-attractors and have no problem acknowledging their existence.

Second, whereas the power-wants are in people, the power-attractors are primarily in your product. To be more accurate, the power-attractors are attributes of your product or of the ways your product is marketed.

Third, the power-wants are expressed mainly through advertising. The power-attractors are expressed through advertising as well, but also through other areas of marketing such as your product/service differences and packaging differences.

POWER-ATTRACTOR NUMBER ONE: FAMILIARITY

Have you ever asked a person what she thinks of a particular product or service, only to get the answer "Never heard of it"? Essentially, the other person is implying that the product or service in question is undesirable or of dubious value. And by what measure? Lack of familiarity.

Conversely, people are naturally attracted to that with which they are most familiar. There are two reasons why this is true:

- **The brain likes to take the easy route.** Remember, your brain works by electrical impulse, just like your toaster, clock radio, or anything else that runs on electricity. And electricity takes the shortest, least resistant route available. With the unfamiliar, the brain first has to make sense of it, evaluate it on some good/bad scale, and file it away in memory. But the brain doesn't have to spend any time or energy processing something with which it is already familiar. So it prefers the familiar over the unfamiliar. Make sense?

- **Familiarity represents less risk.** Most people harbor a natural aversion to risk most of the time.

Familiarity Dominates

But aren't there times when we're attracted to the unfamiliar? Aren't there times a person wants to assume some risk? After all, people want to try new restaurants, see new movies, meet new people, and go on African safaris at times, don't they? Yes, but it takes a conscious effort to seek newness, whereas it takes no conscious effort to gravitate toward the familiar. Natural, subconscious attraction can be overridden when the conscious mind steps in and directs its attention toward the unfamiliar; but familiarity, being primarily governed by the subconscious, dominates most of the time.

Breaking Down the Instinct Barrier

Familiarity also breaks down what we call the *instinct barrier*. Say you suddenly become aware of a particular product or service. You are unfamiliar with it, yet you are asked to make the purchase decision quickly, shortly after your first exposure to it. Unless you consciously override it, your brain will go into a defensive mode and instinctively produce the instinct barrier. Your subconscious mind will choose the more familiar route, which is to do without the product or buy a more familiar brand. In other words, your subconscious mind needs more information—increased familiarity—with the product before it chooses to purchase.

Do you ever find yourself feeling somewhat uncomfortable and hesitant at the time of a purchase decision? It's probably because your brain has produced the instinct barrier. It's telling you to gather more information—become more familiar with the product, service, or seller—before deciding to buy.

How to Build Familiarity

Here are the keys to establishing familiarity:

- **Repeat, repeat, and repeat.** There is almost no practical limit to the number of times your logo or name should appear in your newspaper and magazine ads, in your radio and television commercials, at your promotional events, and in your stores or office.

  I once pointed out to a department store executive that if a person were to be blindfold and taken to his (the executive's) department store, and the blindfold removed in the middle of the men's clothing department, the person could look around all he wanted and still have no idea what store he was in. "But most people don't enter our store blindfolded," he replied. He missed the point. Identifying yourself to those unaware is only part of your objective. Establishing and maintaining familiarity, which comes from repeated exposure to your logo, are the real keys.

- **Use multiple media.** Seeing or hearing from different sources is stronger than seeing or hearing from the same source.

- **A greater number of smaller-sized impressions is more effective than a lesser number of larger-sized impressions.** Making something *smaller sized* means using shorter-length commercials and smaller ad sizes.

Here's an illustration of how familiarity is created through numerous impressions. Let's say you're a sales clerk at a clothing store. On Monday a new customer you've never seen before walks in. We'll call her Jody. She spends 25 minutes in your store, makes a purchase, and leaves. Also on Monday, another customer you've never seen before enters. His name is Bob. He spends five minutes in the store, makes a purchase, and leaves. On Tuesday, Bob returns. He spends another five minutes in the store, purchases, and leaves. On Wednesday, Bob returns again for five minutes before purchasing and leaving. He does the same thing on Thursday and Friday.

Jody has spent 25 minutes in your store this week, and so has Bob. But whom are you most familiar with, Jody or Bob? Notice that you were exposed to each for the same length of time, 25 minutes. But Bob's numerous visits, albeit for shorter lengths of time, increased his familiarity far beyond that of Jody's.

Going with a larger number of smaller-sized ads or shorter-length commercials can stretch your budget. That's why 15-second television commercials are becoming increasingly popular. Even if you have the budget to buy full-page ads or 60-second commercials, you should consider down-sizing and running more of them instead.

- **Use testimonials from familiar people.** You can often establish familiarity more quickly if you use a testimonial from someone with whom the public is already familiar. These third-party endorsers act as conduits for the transfer of familiarity from the third-party endorser to your product.

POWER-ATTRACTOR NUMBER TWO: RESTRAINT

Restraint is the practical application of the "less is more" theory. In marketing, there are many instances when the less availability, time, and space you use, the more attractive your product or service becomes. Let's examine those three dimensions: *availability restraint, time restraint,* and *space restraint.*

Availability Restraint

Restraining availability can increase the perceived value of your product or service. Availability and value are inversely proportional.

What could be more limited in quantity than an art object? In most cases, the rareness of a one-of-a-kind painting or sculpture contributes to its value and demand.

Have you ever seen the print ads for various items from The Franklin Mint? It markets decorative "art" objects such as knives, rings, porcelain cats, swords, old western badges, and goblets. Each of these items is "minted" and "issued" by The Franklin Mint to those who either "subscribe" or "commission" the sale. In most cases, these items are produced in limited quantities.

It used to be you could buy a Parker pen almost anywhere. Discount department stores, drug stores, and supermarkets all had them hanging on the rack. After some of Parker's former executives purchased Parker Pen in 1986, they adopted a new marketing strategy that restrained availability. They pulled out of the discount, drug, and grocery stores. The pens are now sold only in higher-class outlets such as jewelry and office supply stores, and only then under glass—no more rack hanging. The year they bought Parker it lost $500,000. One year later it made a $23.4 million profit.

Limiting your own personal availability can increase your perceived value and subsequent demand. Teens learn the value of limited availability in the dating game. Playing hard to get somehow results in attracting another person. Who wants to date someone who's always available? Restrict your availability, and suddenly interest in you rises.

Which doctor would you choose, one who was available on a moment's notice or one with a five-week advance booking? You might want to see a doctor as soon as possible, but you'd probably have a lot more confidence in the busy one. Actors know that nothing contributes more to their demand than their unavailability. It's the same with attorneys and consultants. And let's not forget about the job candidate. It's always easier to get a job when you already have one. Your occupational attractiveness is highest when you're not even looking.

When MTV banned Madonna's "Justify My Love" video, guess what happened? Radio stations around the country arranged private showings, and people flocked to attend. It became the most-requested video on the Video Jukebox cable channel. Music stores reported record-breaking sales of the video (at $9.98 each) within days of its release.

I'm trying to figure out a way to get this book banned. Nothing, it seems, helps sell a book more than a good banning. Sometimes the mere mention of limited availability, without its actually occurring, is all you need. Victor Ostrovsky's *By Way of Deception* shot to the top of the best-seller lists right after the Israeli government *wanted* it banned in the United States, though no such ban ever materialized.

Availability is one thing, access another. By limiting availability, you increase perceived value and subsequent demand. All that happens *before* the purchase decision. *After* the purchase decision, a person must be able to breeze through the purchase process itself and obtain instant access of the item purchased. This aspect of access almost goes without saying, but you'd be amazed at how many marketers ignore this logic and make it difficult for someone to buy or obtain their product or service.

Ever buy something from Best Products? Once you decide to buy something at a Best Products store, you have to fill out an order blank. Not only do you have to write down your name, address, and phone number each time you purchase something, but you have to write down each item's stock number. To get that number, your have to either look it up in the catalog or find the tag on the display model of the item. That's only the beginning. Next you go to the "order desk" and wait for a clerk to take your order and enter it into the computer. Then you're directed to the "pick up area," where you wait anywhere from 7 to 12 minutes for your item to creep down a conveyor belt and an attendant to call your name. Then you physically take your item to the cashier, where once again you wait in line to pay. No wonder Best declared bankruptcy in 1991. You can be in and out of Kmart half a dozen times for every one trip through the Best Products maze.

Restrict availability to make your product or service more attractive. But once someone makes the purchase decision, make sure he gets instant access.

Time Restraint

When you restrict time, you are essentially saying to the consumer, "We are not here whenever you need us. We are here for a limited amount of time only, after which we will be gone and you will have lost out if you don't act now." The fear of "losing out" on an opportunity can make that opportunity very attractive.

Unfortunately for the marketer, such phrases as "Act now before time runs out," "Limited time offer," and "You have until midnight tonight," are so stale that they have become virtually useless. To make your time restraints effective in the 1990s and beyond, you must make them come as a surprise. You must bring forth a time restraint when it is the last thing one might expect.

No one did that better than George Bush during the 1988 presidential race. In the middle of the second broadcast debate between Bush and Michael Dukakis, Bush was asked if he would agree to another (third) debate. The studio audience applauded the question, reinforcing the widely held sentiment that debates are good and that every self-respecting, image-conscious politician automatically yearns to engage in them. Then Bush stunned everyone by replying, "No. I will not agree to another debate." After the second or two of silence which it took the audience to come out of shock, they gave Bush a thunderous applause. Although the debates had been pretty much even to that point, I believe Bush's unexpected restriction of his time made him the clear-cut winner.

In the record business, exposure of new "product" (songs) on radio and/or music-oriented television shows or cable channels is essential. Record companies spend a lot of time and money promoting their material to the radio and television programming people who decide what songs to play. They do all they can to convince these programmers to give their product some airplay.

So how does a record company virtually guarantee itself a ton of airplay with little effort on its own part? By turning the tables through an unexpected time restraint. Here's how it works: When a relatively "hot" artist releases a new album, the record company will sometimes restrict airplay by declaring an official "release date," before which the song or album "may not be played on air." What happens when you tell radio people they can't play a song or album? They scramble to get hold of it and play it. They obtain advance copies leaked from mysterious, unnamed sources. They go to whatever length it takes to get it on the air before the official release date (so as to beat competing stations). In many cases, the record company even issues the offending stations a cease-and-desist order or threatens a lawsuit. At any rate, by simply placing a time restraint on the front end (as opposed to a back-end time restraint, which cuts off availability at some point), the company is virtually assured of mass airplay.

Do you know why absence makes the heart grow fonder? Could it be because someone has restricted the amount of time he or she is spending with another? It's been said the reserve quarterback is the most popular guy on the team. His popularity is inversely proportional to his playing time, or on-the-field exposure.

Everyone loved the Lone Ranger. He breezed into town, saved the day, and got out before anyone had the chance to think less of him. If you followed him back to his favorite rock, or wherever he lived, and had to watch him do his laundry, cook rabbit stew, and complain about his aching back, would his mystique have dwindled any? The Lone Ranger was a master of time restraint, knowing that his absence made him all the more attractive.

How has Michael Jackson maintained his high level of popularity in three different decades? By restricting his time in the public eye. He produces a new album every four or five years, does a tour, then fades back into the woodwork. Except for a few, brief appearances here and there, he's all but invisible most of the time. The press even refers to him as "the reclusive Michael Jackson."

Space Restraint

If you give people too much physical space, they'll think there's something wrong. Restrict the amount of space and people become attracted. Sound strange? Consider this: You and your friends, headed for an exciting night on the town, narrow your choice of nightclubs down to two. Nightclub A is packed with people by 9 P.M., when you arrive. In fact, people are standing in line to get in. It is definitely "happening." Nightclub B across the street has plenty of room inside. No line. It appears dead. Which do you choose?

Most people would choose A over B. Nightclub A appears to be where the action is; nightclub B appears to be actionless. Yet both nightclubs had the same number of people, 200, in attendance when you checked them out. Why, then, did A appear livelier than B? Simple. Nightclub A was physically smaller and held only 200 people, so the place was packed. B was a much larger facility, with a capacity of 600, so it appeared practically empty. Remember power-want number four? People want what others want. And when you restrict the physical space, you can create that condition.

Think about perfume or cologne. I'm sure you've noticed that the most expensive and desirable brands give you very little of the actual product in the bottle. By restricting the physical space—designing the bottle to hold very little liquid— the manufacturers raise its attractiveness.

In years past, physically large products used to be more attractive than smaller products. The proliferation of the microchip has altered people's perceptions in recent years, however. With electronic gadgets and computers becoming more powerful as they become physically smaller, the perceived relationship between size and value—in many areas besides electronics—has become inversely related. There are exceptions, of course, but there's a good chance your product's attractiveness can increase as its size decreases.

POWER-ATTRACTOR NUMBER THREE: DISTANCE/PROXIMITY

This power-attractor has to do with the geographic origin of your product or service.

In some cases, the farther away from the potential buyer's home town your product's perceived origin, the more attractive it becomes. The strange way in which people place lofty value on items of distant origin is illustrated by an old story of an American tourist in Mexico. He comes across a "one-of-a-kind" vase and pays the street merchant 30 American dollars for it, having haggled the price down from $150. After the tourist is out of sight, the merchant goes in the back and pulls an identical vase out of a crate and puts it on display. It turns out the merchant buys them in bulk from some Asian wholesaler at $1.70 each. Although Mr. Tourist could have bought the same thing at his hometown department store for about six bucks, which would he feel more comfortable displaying in his home? The one from Mexico or the one from down the street?

The word *imported* attached to some items (or simply implied) makes them immediately more attractive. Häagen-Dazs ice cream is a domestic brand. In fact, it's been around for over 30 years, which makes it a traditional domestic brand. But its name makes it sound imported. Most people think it is.

Although my consulting firm is located in Richmond, Virginia, most of our clients are in other cities, other states. Why? In the consulting business, the farther we travel to get to a client, the more valuable our advice is perceived to be.

If you had a choice of two brands of beer, one brewed near your hometown and the other brewed halfway across the country, which would you choose? Before Coors went national, people in parts of the country in which Coors was unavailable used to treat it like some rare delicacy. They'd bring it back from a Denver vacation or have it shipped to them by friends. To some, even a beer from across the country isn't good enough. If it isn't brewed in Mexico, Canada, or Germany, they're not attracted.

In other cases, the closer your product's origin to where it is purchased and consumed, the more attractive it is.

Most politicians have no chance of winning if they haven't spent years living in the jurisdiction in which they seek election. No community wants an "outsider" to show up and tell them how to run their community.

Proximity is everything when it comes to sports. I've often thought it's interesting that so many people in Richmond, Virginia, attach themselves to the Washington Redskins, even through Richmond and Washington are separate cities 100 miles apart and have nothing to do with one another. But Washington is the closest city with an NFL franchise, so people in Richmond are attracted.

Can you take advantage of either proximity or distance appeal? Not every marketer can, but you may be able to find a way if you think creatively.

POWER-ATTRACTOR NUMBER FOUR: A GOOD DEAL

I noted in the last chapter that people want to own things that cost a lot of money because high-priced goods and services provide status. However, that doesn't mean people actually want to *pay* a high price. They want to own a high-priced item, but they want to pay as little as possible to get it. In other words, they want a good deal.

Let's review for a moment how a high price contributes to attractiveness. A $600 suit is better, and therefore more desirable, than a $300 suit, wouldn't you say? A $35,000 car is better and more desirable than a $16,000 car. A $35 bottle of perfume is better and more desirable than a $7 bottle (even when you get four times as much of the cheaper stuff). An accounting firm that charges $150 an hour must be better, and therefore more desirable, than one that charges $50 an hour.

Likewise, the word "expensive" often works for you, not against you. People are proud of the fact that they drive an *expensive* car, that they eat in *expensive* restaurants, that they stay at *expensive* hotels, that they wear *expensive* clothes, that they receive an *expensive* gift on Valentine's day, and that they have an *expensive* law firm on their case. People flaunt the fact that they have expensive things. Expensive products and services are not a turn-off, they're desirable! (Be careful how you use the word *inexpensive*. Don't assume that something inexpensive is automatically attractive.)

Now let's examine how a high price works against you. People never feel good about buying something if they believe they can get the same thing for less elsewhere. (That's why a high-priced item must be of top quality and significantly different.) Also, many people enjoy the process of finding or negotiating "good deals." To some, the buying process is a game they like to play and win.

The Expensive-Deal Strategy

Your objective, therefore, is to use a high price to heighten attractiveness, yet sell at a lower price to give people a good deal. We call this the *Expensive-Deal Strategy*. When you implement the Expensive-Deal Strategy, you have the most powerful pricing structure possible in effect.

Here are the guidelines for implementing the Expensive-Deal Strategy:

- **For high-ticket items, or when consumers buy irregularly (less than once a year), discount your price.** Automobile dealers, for example, have been following this strategy for years. Furniture and appliance retailers are always having a sale of one kind or another, almost never selling at the "regular" price. And few people ever sell a home without coming down from the original asking price. The advantages you gain from discounting or negotiating price outweigh the disadvantages when people buy irregularly.

- **For small-ticket items, or when consumers buy regularly (more than once a year), maintain price.** Maintaining price integrity is important if your consumers or customers buy frequently. Otherwise, you condition your customers to haggle over price or hold off buying until the next inevitable sale occurs. Even walking away from unfavorable deals strengthens your position in most cases.

- **Use creative deal packaging.** The way to maintain your price integrity and still give your customers a good deal is to package in ways that accomplish both objectives.

There are an infinite number of ways you can package your deal. Buy three, get one free; buy one, get a second at half price; commit to buying x number over the next year, get a volume discount; buy before the end of the month, get 10 percent more at no charge; buy item A at the regular price, get item B at a discount. You get the idea.

Use your imagination to package creatively. An optometrist decided to offer $20 for any old pair of glasses traded in with the purchase of a new pair. He could have simply discounted his price of new glasses by $20, but it wouldn't have been nearly as effective. With the $20 trade-in allowance, he was able to maintain price integrity and give his customers a great deal by recognizing the equity value in a pair of old glasses. I personally saw the results of this clever package: two large cartons full of old glasses and an equal number of new glasses sold. It worked like a charm.

Some radio stations have a hard time selling commercials to air in the midnight-to-6 A.M. time period. So they creatively package as follows: Buy x number of commercials (called "spots") in the 6 A.M.-to-midnight time period, and for only 10 percent more money, you'll get an equal number of spots in the midnight-to-6 A.M. time period. Not only does this fill up commercial "availabilities" in the midnight-to-6 A.M. period, it brings in additional revenue. And the client gets a good deal.

Automobile manufacturers and dealers are great packagers. They offer rebates, low financing, options packages, trade-in allowances, and so on. Learn from them and create your own packages. Just follow the philosophy of the Expensive-Deal Strategy: Use a high price to create attractiveness, and then offer packages to give the buyer a good deal.

POWER-ATTRACTOR CHECKLIST

Run each of your ads, commercials, promotions, and contests through this check list. More than likely, you won't be able to use all of the power-attractors all the time, but one or two is all you need to make a big difference.

1. Are you building familiarity by constantly exposing your logo as often as possible? If you have a physical location, can patrons see your logo wherever they look?
2. Can you restrict your product's or service's availability somewhat? Can you suddenly and surprisingly restrict the time alloted to purchase your item? Is the nature of your product such that making it smaller increases its perceived value?
3. Can you play up the local or distant origin of your product? Can you create consumer loyalty by pitting your locally produced item against "foreign" competition? Can you create an aura or mystique by emphasizing the exotic, distant origin of your item?
4. Are you attaching a relatively high price to your product or service, yet creatively packaging it so that buyers get a good deal?

Chapter Seven

Putting People into Decision Making Mode

I t's time for a quiz. Relax, it's multiple choice. There are no right or wrong answers. I just want to determine what mood you're in right now.

Question: Based on your present mood, which one of the following activities would you rather do right now, assuming you had to put this book down and engage in one of them?

A. Play a round of golf (or any other sport you like).

B. Call a friend and chit-chat on the phone.

C. Pop a tape into your VCR and watch a movie.

D. Go to the mall and shop for some new clothes.

If you chose either A or D, you're in Decision Making Mode, or DMM. Engaging in any sporting activity requires concentration and many instantaneous decisions on your brain's part. Shopping requires perhaps less concentration and not-so-instantaneous decisions, but decisions none the less.

If you chose either B or C, you're out of DMM at the moment. Neither chatting with a friend nor watching a movie requires a string of decisions. Your brain's decision-making function can take a rest when you engage in either of these activities. (Technically, all activity requires the brain to make decisions. But some decisions, like those required to chat with a friend or watch a movie, are so easy they require very little decision-making thought, so we don't count them.)

TO DECIDE OR NOT TO DECIDE

The brain likes to avoid any unnecessary activity as a means of self-preservation. It tries to expend the least amount of energy to accomplish its tasks and will therefore take the easier route whenever possible. Making decisions requires more brain activity than not making decisions. The natural tendency is for the brain to avoid DMM, since DMM is work. Kicking the brain into DMM usually requires some expenditure of energy to begin with, and even more executing the subsequent decisions.

That doesn't mean the brain is always trying to avoid DMM. Sometimes the brain wants to be in DMM. This happens when the resulting feeling, let's say emotional stimulation, is greater and more pleasurable than the work it takes—the decisions one must make—to generate it. That's why you enjoy getting on the golf course and making all those decisions . . . it's fun.

There are times when you feel like making decisions and times when you don't. You're in DMM at times, and out of DMM at times. Your brain shifts between the two modes, directing you to engage in decision-making activity or non-decision-making activity to keep you comfortably balanced.

THE SIGNIFICANCE OF DMM

A person must be in DMM in order to make a purchase decision. That is not exactly the same thing as saying that a person is in DMM each time he makes a purchase. He could, after all, decide to purchase a product on Monday, but not get around to making the purchase till Friday. At the time he actually makes the purchase, he may well be out of DMM. The act of purchasing is not really that important. It's the purchase decision, which precedes the act, that counts.

Speaking of the time lag between the purchase decision and the actual act of purchasing, isn't that really what a *buying habit* is? A buying habit is nothing more than an old decision that is repeatedly acted upon sometime after the original decision has been made. I'll bet you know someone that shops at the same grocery store week after week, month after month, year after year. At one time that person was in DMM with regard to grocery shopping. She made a decision; she chose a store to patronize. After that, she drops out of DMM with regard to grocery stores and simply keeps acting upon the old decision over and over.

Buying habits are good for the marketer. They help protect you from having your consumers or customers snaked by a competitor. Yes, it works the other way around, too. You must often break a buying habit to get a new customer. But with all the ammunition you're getting from this book, you'll be breaking buying habits right and left.

One more point before we move on: Simply because a person is in DMM doesn't necessarily mean he will choose to purchase your product or service. He may choose to purchase your competitor's product or none at all. In DMM, a purchase decision of some kind will be made. The outcome of that decision is not significant at the moment. For now, just be aware that a person must be in DMM in order to buy your product or service.

HOW MARKETING AND DMM RELATE

When a person's brain is in DMM with regard to your particular product or service, it is ready and willing to make a purchase decision. But that doesn't occur very often. Most of the time a person is out of DMM with regard to any particular product or service.

I have a question for you. If most people are out of DMM most of the time, what good does it do you to market to them? A marketing message that reaches someone out of DMM is a wasted message, isn't it? Yes, it is true most of your marketing messages will reach people who are out of DMM at the time. No, such an impression is not wasted. When people are out of DMM, their brains are still receiving information. They're susceptible to influence, just not ready to make a buying decision yet.

In the previous chapter, and later in this book, I talk about penetrating the subconscious mind and making impressions. Most of this happens when the receiver is out of DMM. But the impressions are made nevertheless, and they mount up. The cumulative effect of numerous impressions received out of DMM can cause the brain to *kick into* DMM.

In addition, your accumulated marketing impressions are preconditioning the receiver to choose your product or service when his brain does shift into DMM. That's really what top-of-mind awareness is all about. Whatever brand you recall first when your brain kicks into DMM is very likely to be the brand that made the most significant impression back when you were out of DMM.

Timing is a factor. Since purchase decisions occur only when people are in DMM, and since (a) DMM regarding a particular product or service occurs infrequently, and (b) different people go into DMM at different times, there may be a time lag between your marketing activity and the sales results it produces. This is to be expected.

Many times marketers will engage in trial-and-error marketing— try something and see if results come in. If there are no results, abandon the marketing plan and try something else. They never give their campaign a chance to germinate. Results don't always show up immediately after you begin marketing. Results show up when people are in DMM. That's why it may take a number of impressions, over a period of time, for effectiveness to kick in and results to show.

INSTIGATING DMM IS ONE OF YOUR MARKETING OBJECTIVES

In order for one to purchase your product or service, he or she must first be in DMM at some point prior to the actual purchase behavior. Therefore, one of your ongoing goals is to instigate

DMM. By instigating DMM, purchases can happen faster and in greater volume.

Keep in mind, however, that putting people into DMM is not necessarily the same thing as causing them to choose your product or service. Ideally, they will choose your product or service. But instigating DMM does not guarantee that people will choose your or anyone's product or service. It merely means they are ready and willing to make some kind of decision in that regard.

Think of the purchase of your product or service as a three-step mental process. The first step occurs when an individual's brain goes into DMM. The second step occurs when the individual chooses a particular brand. The third step occurs when he or she makes the actual purchase decision. Since choosing your brand and making the purchase decision must be preceded by the brain going into DMM, let's deal with just that function for now. Let's see how you can instigate DMM. (Getting people to choose your brand and make the actual purchase decision is addressed in other chapters.)

DMM STIMULI

What causes the brain to go into and out of DMM? Dropping out of DMM is the brain's natural state. It will automatically go there in the absence of any DMM-activating stimuli. It will also go there immediately following a decision.

There are five types of DMM-activating stimuli that cause the brain to go into DMM. Two are out of the marketer's control. The other three can be brought about or enhanced through good marketing.

What the Marketer Cannot Affect

- **Acute need.** Your television set breaks down, so it's time to buy a new one. Your food supply is running low, so off you go to the grocery store. Your wardrobe needs updating, so you decide it's time to go shopping. Your car has seen better days, so it's time to buy a newer one.

In these cases, it's the growing or sudden need to acquire a necessity, defined by the consumer, that activates DMM. The marketer can't affect such decisions; you can't control when someone runs out of shampoo.

- **Periodic self-activation.** Rarely does a person make a decision once and continue acting on it ever afterward. Even without any outside stimuli, a person usually reactivates DMM with regard to a particular product or service periodically.

   This particular DMM-activating stimulus is internal and is not one you can affect. But noting its existence tells you that people will consider buying your product or service on occasion anyway, even if you do very little to instigate DMM. Notice I said they'll *consider* buying your item. I didn't say they'll buy it.

What the Marketer Can Affect

- **Collected impressions.** As I mentioned earlier, the cumulative weight of a number of persuasive impressions received out of DMM can cause the brain to kick into DMM. Like the drops of water that accumulate in a precariously balanced bucket, one more drop and the entire bucket tips over.

   The latest direct mail campaign, the latest billboard campaign, or the latest television, radio, or print campaign executed may very well be the drop of water that causes the entire bucket to tip. You've kicked many people into DMM at once, and your sales gush forth. This happens quite often to marketers that maintain a healthy dose of marketing activity on a regular basis. They've got enough people with full buckets out there who only need one more drop to kick into DMM.

   But marketers who do not engage in a healthy amount of marketing activity on a regular basis do not benefit from the effects of collected impressions, because no impressions are collecting in people's minds. Once every two years such marketers do some ad or promotional campaign and get disappointing results. That's because they're only filling buckets, not tipping any over.

Remember when we talked about bursting through the results threshold in Chapter 4? We said that to get results, you must do it big. Now you know why. Ninety-five percent of the marketing you do fills the bucket—it builds upon itself—and is therefore valuable, but it may not be enough to activate DMM in many people. Five percent of the marketing you do is the final drop that activates DMM and makes 100 percent of your expenditures effective.

Collected impressions are very potent. They produce results, even though the results don't always show up immediately. Some people have empty buckets—you've got to do a good deal of filling before they'll tip over. Understanding this will prevent you from uprooting or cancelling your marketing activity during certain times when it may appear results are not forthcoming.

- **Emotional stimulation.** Sometimes a buying habit can become too comfortable. It can become dull and boring. When an alternative stimulates the emotions through advertising in a way that the habit does not, DMM can become activated. If this weren't true, very few married people would get divorced. After all, once one says "I do," the brain is supposed to drop out of DMM with regard to mating. But when the brain is lacking the type of emotional stimulation it craves, it will be most receptive to another alternative that supplies the desired stimulation.

- **A new or different outcome.** People will go into DMM when they perceive that a new or different outcome is possible. Something new or different can break a buying habit and snap a person into DMM.

Why are laundry detergent marketers always sticking the words "New" and "Improved" on their boxes? They're telling us that the outcome, presumably a cleaner or brighter wash, is different from what it used to be.

Earlier I said the marketer can't control when the consumer runs out of shampoo or when his or her television set breaks down. But by introducing something new, something technically advanced or of a newer style or design, you can often activate DMM before an acute need would otherwise activate it.

HOW TO INSTIGATE DMM

Here are the two things you should do on an ongoing basis:

- **Step 1: Maintain marketing activity.** When you keep up a steady dose of powerful marketing activity, you empower each individual advertisement, commercial, promotion, piece of publicity, and contest to produce immediate results. Each lays on top of the cumulated weight of the others and each acts as the final drop that activates DMM in many people at once.

- **Step 2: Periodically improve or change some aspects of your product's performance.** In most cases, you must periodically improve or advance your product or service, not only to keep your existing consumers or customers from deserting, but also constantly to be kicking others into DMM so they'll try your product or service.

Chapter Eight

The Power
of Projection

The last time you purchased a new car, did you test drive it beforehand? And the last time you bought a new suit, dress, or coat, did you try it on first? The last time you bought a piece of furniture, did you imagine what it would look like in your home before you decided to buy it? And the last time you decided where to vacation, did you imagine what it would be like to be there before you decided to go?

Yes, yes, yes, and yes. But why? Let's take them one at a time. Why did you test drive the car before buying? To determine how it runs and handles, of course. But that was only part of the reason. Actually, you test drove the car mainly to help your brain experience the *feelings* you would get if you owned it. You wanted to experience what it would *feel like* when other people on the road saw you in the car... when your neighbors saw it parked in your driveway... when your co-workers saw you getting into it and out of it in the parking lot. You imagined what it would *feel like* to experience these things. Actually climbing into the car and taking it for a spin helped you do so.

When you tried on a suit or dress, you did so to determine how well it fit and whether or not it looked good on you. But another reason you tried it on was to create the *feelings* you would experience wearing the item to work, to a social function, or wherever.

SAMPLE THE FEELING

The brain has an insatiable desire to produce *sample feelings*. That is, it produces certain feelings ahead of time that actually represent the future feelings it would experience if one owned the item in question.

Think about it. When you shop for furniture, don't you imagine how each piece would look in your home? Don't you try to feel what it would be like to have each piece in your home, and even how you would feel when others see the furniture in your home? How about vacation sites? Don't you base your choice on your feelings as you imagine what it would be like to be there?

ENVISIONING IS THE BRAIN'S FAVORITE SPORT

Your brain attempts to produce sample feelings before each and every decision you make, including each purchase decision. Sample feelings, after all, are a great tool to aid in your decision-making process.

The method your brain uses to produce sample feelings is a process called *envisioning*.

Envisioning something is like watching a movie in which the person doing the envisioning is the lead character. The obvious difference between watching a real movie with your eyes and envisioning one in your mind is that the envisioned movie really doesn't exist. It's a mental mirage created by the brain to produce sample feelings.

Most of the envisioning your brain does is done at the subconscious level. You don't even know you're doing it most of the time. Like the last time you walked by the fresh fruit aisle and decided to put a bunch of bananas in the cart. The mental vision of you and/or your family eating and enjoying the bananas happened so fast and so far below your level of consciousness you were totally unaware of it. But it happened nonetheless. If the vision hadn't been created, and a positive sample feeling experienced, your brain wouldn't have instructed you to buy the bananas.

PROJECTION AIDS ENVISIONING

As a marketer, you want people to envision owning your product or service. You want them to experience sample feeling so pleasurable and strong that they feel compelled to buy.

You foster envisioning of your product or service through the technique called *projection*. Projecting a vision is like showing a mental movie—a movie you produced as you saw fit—a movie that shows your product or service in use by the prospective buyer—a movie that helps the prospect envision and produce positive sample feelings.

Because sample feelings play such a strong role in the purchase decision process, projection is an extremely effective marketing technique. Moreover, projection runs into virtually no resistance by the receiver. A person's mind is wide open for as much projection as you care to supply. That's because people want to envision; they do it all the time. And projection aids the envisioning process. Working together, not in opposition, the marketer and consumer are on the same side—as is the case with every single demand-creating technique I discuss in this book.

When you project an image, you are painting a mental picture for the prospect to see and experience. Through projection, you take a person on a mental trip into the future, a future that includes the ownership of your product or service and the resulting feeling.

Projection is most often achieved through advertising. It is created by the ways you word your copy or dialog and how you compose your photos or pictures. This will become clear as we discuss how to implement projection.

HOW TO USE PROJECTION IN YOUR ADVERTISING

Projection is not a difficult technique to implement. Here's how to use projection in your advertising:

- **Step 1. Depict one or more people experiencing the feelings one gets through either actual product usage or as a result of product usage.** Here are some examples for randomly selected products and services:

    Boat. Without projection: Show the boat as it appears in the showroom or parked at a dock. Projection: Depict people having the time of their lives, laughing and screaming with excitement in your boat while it is moving in the water.

    Perfume. Without projection: Show a woman putting on perfume in front of the mirror. Projection: Show a woman out on the town attracting male attention or in the company of an adoring male.

    Radio station. Without Projection: Show pictures of your personalities or news events the station has covered. Projection: Show people listening at work, in the car, and at home. Show people winning your contest while listening.

    Legal services. Without projection: Show the senior partner sitting at her desk or talking about her services. Projection: Show a judge declaring "judgment for the plaintiff!" and a client jumping with joy and hugging the attorney.

    House paint. Without projection: Show a homeowner painting his house. Projection: Show a homeowner beaming as he and a neighbor look over his freshly painted house.

    Politician. Without projection: Talk about what a dirty rotten scoundrel your opponent is. With projection: Show happy people who have benefited from improvements you made once in office.

• **Step 2. Word your copy in after-the-fact fashion, as though the reader already owns your product or service.** Here are some examples:

Without projection: "Come experience the beauty and serenity of an Alaskan vacation." Projection: "In Alaska, you are surrounded by beauty and bathed in serenity."

Without projection: "Tune in Wednesday night at 9 for 'Jake and the Fatman.'" Projection: "You'll see 'Jake and the Fatman' Wednesday night at 9."

Without projection: "Come see our fine selection of Acme washers and dryers, on sale now through Sunday." Projection: "Your new Acme washer and dryer are on sale now through Sunday."

THINK PROJECTION

The effects of projection can be striking. Yet using projection in your advertising is quite simple. Just think about projection when you compose your photography and word your copy. Most of the time a few simple structural adjustments in your video and copy make the vast difference between projection and no projection.

PART 3

IGNITING DEMAND

In Part 1, you built your marketing jet. In Part 2, you taxied down the runway. Now you're about to lift off.

Marketers often have difficulty getting demand started, usually because they are unaware of or haven't implemented most the things we've talked about to this point. Other times it's because they aren't sure what specific actions to take to ignite the spark. Chapters 9 through 12 contain the sparks that ignite demand. When you implement the techniques presented in this part, you'll begin to see the demand needle move.

Chapter Nine
Triggering the Purchase Decision

I s it possible for you to do all the things we've discussed in the first eight chapters, to build a great deal of want and desire, yet still not sell much product? Is it possible for a team to play a great game and still lose? Not only is it possible, but also it happens quite often. A marketer makes all the right moves, but the payoff never arrives. "The operation was a success but the patient died" type of thing.

This is something you can avoid very easily once you know how. Then you can be confident your class-A marketing effort will translate into the kind of results you so richly deserve.

LATENT AND ACTIVE WANT

Wanting something doesn't automatically mean you'll buy it, unless you're under 15 years of age. At some age fiscal responsibility begins to take hold (although for some people that time never arrives). As one grows into adulthood, one increasingly separates want from the purchase decision. You may want a lot of things, but you don't run out and purchase them all just because you want them.

There are two types of want or desire, *latent* and *active*. Latent want occurs when a person decides he wants something (usually a subconscious function) but doesn't go so far as to decide to make the purchase. "I want a new Thunderbird," his mind says to itself. Active want happens when the person goes one step further and decides to make the purchase (usually a conscious function). "I want a new Thunderbird, and I'm going down to Joe Doe Ford to buy one!"

To create real demand, the kind that ultimately results in burgeoning sales, you must convert latent want into active want. I call this conversion the *triggering* of the purchase decision.

Think of a person's mind as a river. Want for your particular product or service which intensifies in her mind is like the water accumulating on one side of a dam. The intensification of want is like the increase of water pressure. The water pressure may be building, but the water still isn't flowing (she hasn't decided to make the purchase). And it won't flow until the dam gates open.

THE LOGIC TRIGGER

The trigger that converts latent want into active want is *logic*. You build the intensity of want and desire primarily through the use of emotion, and you trigger the purchase decision through logic. Like building the water pressure, then opening the gate.

Many people believe the subconscious mind is the logical one and the conscious mind is the emotional one. Actually, it's just the opposite. The subconscious mind determines whether you want something or not, the conscious mind determines whether you go out and buy that something or not.

A purchase decision, therefore, is primarily a conscious function. And the conscious mind thrives on logic. If it doesn't have one or more strong, logical reasons for purchasing, it won't make the purchase decision. And it's up to you, the marketer, to provide that logic. Otherwise, a person will find it much easier to forgo purchasing your item than expending the brain power necessary to concoct logical reasons for purchasing.

HOW LOGIC WORKS

What gives logic its power to trigger a purchase decision? There are three factors:

- **Logic aids communication.** It's immensely easier to explain things in logical terms than in emotional terms. For years there was a running joke among the television production crew of "American Bandstand." They knew that practically every time Dick Clark would ask some teens to rate a new song, the chances were they'd say, "It's got a nice beat and you can dance to it." It may have been much more accurate for a person to say, "The specific integration of vocal and musical sounds in this song induces an emotional reaction in my brain that I find highly pleasurable on the subconscious level, Mr. Clark." But what are the chances of that answer popping up?

  When you purchase something, you want to be able to talk about it. And it's a lot easier to talk about things in logical terms. If the logic of your purchase or of the product itself is lacking, your brain will find it difficult to make the purchase decision.

- **Logic averts ridicule.** Most of our purchase decisions are potential targets for question or ridicule. When someone questions the wisdom behind your purchase of that new, expensive sports car, which of the following answers sounds flakier and more subject to ridicule, and which sounds more justifiable and sound? "I'm trying to impede my growing feelings of inadequacy by bolstering my perceived sexual attractiveness," or "This baby is maintenance-free and has a great resale value." There's nothing like a strong dose of logical reasoning to squelch a doubter. Remember: Emotion fuels debate, logic settles debate.

People will repeat what they're told. When you provide logic in your advertising, you're giving the receivers the ammunition they need to justify and defend the purchase decision. That makes it a lot easier for them to make the purchase.

- **Logic suppresses guilt.** Some people harbor feelings of guilt that become activated when they make a purchase based strictly on emotion. The purchase produces contradictory feelings, as one force—emotional gratification—is pleasurable, and the resulting force—guilt—is painful. The two feelings struggle against each other, producing anxiety and stress in the individual. The brain searches for a way to end the internal conflict, or better yet, to avoid it in the first place. As a result, the purchase is not made.

Logic suppresses feelings of guilt. When enough logic exists, guilt is averted, and the purchase decision can be made.

EMOTION–LOGIC CONFLICT

Each of us experiences an inherent and recurring conflict between our emotional and logical minds. Guilt suppression is an example of this *emotion-logic conflict* which exists in each of our brains. Left unabated, emotion-logic conflict will often inhibit a person from making a purchase decision as a way of suppressing guilt feelings associated with the purchase.

Let's take a closer look at emotion-logic conflict so you'll be better able to counteract its effects. Have you or anyone you know ever expressed conflicts like these?

"I really want this new stereo system (emotion), but my wife would kill me if I bought it (logic)."

"I know I should save my money (logic), but you only live once (emotion)!"

"This dress is me (emotion), but if I take the time to check other stores I may find something just as nice for less (logic)."

Purchase-inhibiting emotion-logic conflicts also exist between individuals as well as in the minds of single individuals. Here are some examples:

PERSON ONE: "This house is great! Let's make an offer (emotion)!"
PERSON TWO: "I really think we should look at more houses before we jump to one (logic)."

PERSON ONE: "Wouldn't this hot sports car be great (emotion)!?"
PERSON TWO: "There's no trunk space, and not enough protection if you're in an accident (logic)."

PERSON ONE: "Let's go to Maui (emotion)!"
PERSON TWO: "We'd have to go over the budget and see if we could afford it (logic)."

These are all outward expressions of emotion-logic conflicts, though the conflicts themselves occur at the subconscious level. People are seldom consciously aware of the actual emotion-logic conflicts that go on in their brains, though they are often aware of the resulting feelings of discomfort, stress, or anxiety.

Both the emotional and logical minds want to have influence over your purchases, and often they don't agree. That's why emotion-logic conflict inhibits the purchase decision. In a person's brain, the displeasurable feelings of discomfort, stress, or anxiety caused by emotion-logic conflict are linked to the purchase in a cause-and-effect manner, as though the purchase causes the discomfort. Since the brain wants to avoid discomfort, it directs the person to avoid the purchase.

When you present logic-based as well as emotion-based persuasion in your advertising, you're giving both the logical and emotional minds some gratification. And when the two minds are satisfied, they'll stop conflicting. Then the subsequent purchase sails through without opposition, much like a bill moving through Congress when both the House and Senate agree.

HOW TO USE LOGIC TO TRIGGER
THE PURCHASE DECISION

Every advertisement and commercial you produce should contain some emotion-based persuasion and some logic-based persuasion. You know why. Emotion produces want and logic triggers it. You need both. Here are the procedures:

- **Step 1. Use a 9:1 emotion:logic ratio.** Or another way of looking at it: 90 percent of each ad or commercial you construct should be devoted to emotion-intensive information, 10 percent to logic-intensive information. Why such an imbalance between the two? It takes a good deal of effort to build want, but it only takes a small amount of effort to trigger it.

  Example: Pontiac's "We Build Excitement" campaign mentioned earlier uses both emotion and logic in the 9:1 ratio. In the television version, the car moves down water-slicked roads in exotic locations while youthful members of both sexes interact. Energetic, contemporary music contributes to the electric mood. All of this is the emotional part. Then at the very end, the highway/city miles-per-gallon information is presented. In some cases the factory financing or rebates available are mentioned. This is the logical information. The emotional part produces desire, and the logical part provides the reasoning one needs to justify and *act upon* the desire.

- **Step 2. Present emotion first, logic second.** Remember the sequence: Build want with emotion, then trigger it with logic.

- **Step 3. Use wording that is easy to repeat.** You want to spoon-feed logic to the receivers in a manner that makes it easy for them to spit it back . . . word for word. Use wording that is easy to remember and easy to repeat verbally.

  Radio stations do this all the time. Lines like "We play the kind of music everyone at work can agree on" enable a person to use that very line in conversation when debating what station he and his co-workers should tune to. "Let's listen to Q102 . . . they play the kind of music we can all agree on," he's likely to say. Even when the need to repeat a line of logic verbally does not arise, a person will still repeat the line in her mind, using it to convince herself.

To foster verbalization, your logic statements should be short and quick. This is not the time to be cute or clever. Don't play with the receiver's mind. Just make it straight and quick.

• **Step 4. Justify the emotion in your copy.** If your commercial or ad is successful in arousing the receiver's emotions, the receiver will likely develop some degree of emotion-logic conflict. Therefore, your logic statement(s) must negate the conflict to make your ad highly effective.

A person's logical mind will oppose the very same emotion it is experiencing at any given moment. You must provide a logical reason why the emotion is justified.

Say you design the emotional portion of your ad to arouse the emotion of joy or excitement. Then you know the receiver's logical mind will oppose the emotion by reasoning that experiencing the emotion through the use of your product or service is too irresponsible or hedonistic an activity to engage in, or the like. So part of the logic you present might be a line or two that says "You work hard and deserve a little fun" or "Hard work deserves reward." The idea is to negate the logical mind's objection by giving it something it will agree with.

Your emotion-justifying line(s) may simply be one or two sentences contained in the body of your copy, as the above example indicates. Or it could be contained in your slogan. McDonald's "You Deserve a Break Today" campaign/slogan is one example. Miller Beer's "Now It's Miller Time" campaign/slogan is another. In Miller's case, they know people can have a hard time justifying feeling the excitement and joy of consuming alcohol. So they show people working, then enjoying a beer after work. Hey, you work hard, so drinking beer is justified. Your logical mind agrees and you make the purchase decision.

Chapter Ten

Pre-Process
for Instant Impact

A s one of my clients recently observed, "It's not easy making an impact. We can say whatever we want, and it either goes in one ear and out the other...or it never even goes in one ear at all!" Such are the woes of our "over-communicated" society.

How do you make a significant impact on people when they're "selectively perceiving" only a small percentage of the marketing messages that reach them? The answer to that question is the subject of this chapter. You are about to learn of a simple psychological technique that has the power to get your message past a person's perception filters and make a strong impact— *instantly*.

And that's not all. In addition to making an instant, strong impact, you'll be able to arrange things so that your brand name is recalled instantly whenever a person first thinks of whatever type of product or service you market. You no longer have to spend decades working to achieve top-of-mind awareness. You can obtain stellar results in a relatively short time.

THE BRAIN'S INFORMATION PROCESSING SYSTEM

To learn how to achieve both instant impact and instant recall, you must first understand how the brain handles information.

As each of the five senses—sight, hearing, touch, taste, and smell—receives information (which happens constantly), it instantaneously sends the information to the brain. The brain then decides what to do with that information. As a result of these decisions, your information—your name or logo, for example—either makes an instant, strong impact, or it makes a delayed, weak impact, or it makes no impact. Unfortunately for most marketers, their name or logo makes either a weak impact or no impact most of the time. For you, that is about to change.

How Processing Works

Say a person sees your logo in a print ad. That piece of information, your logo, travels through nerves from the eyes to the brain. When it arrives, the brain tries to determine what your logo or name *means*. The search for meaning is what we call *processing*.

To process your logo or name, the brain begins performing a specific, one- or two-step maneuver to determine meaning. Once it has determined meaning, it stops processing. Let's walk through the steps so you can see exactly how processing is accomplished.

1. You see the word "Brensello's" on a sign along the highway. (I made up the word for purposes of this illustration. Any similarity with an actual person, place, company, or product is coincidental and should be ignored.) In its quest for meaning, your brain begins processing the word "Brensello's" by executing step one: searching its memory for information that matches. In other words, it looks for some degree of familiarity. If this latest piece of information—the most recent sighting of the word "Brensello's"—matches up with any stored information in your memory, *your brain will assign the same meaning to the new information as the stored meaning from its memory bank.* For example, you recall having

eaten at Brensello's; your memory indicates it's a submarine sandwich shop. Therefore, the latest sighting of the word "Brensello's" has been assigned a meaning, and processing stops.

Everything that has happened so far, from seeing the word "Brensello's" to searching your memory, discovering a match and assigning a meaning, took place at the subconscious level, and in a split second. Reread the previous paragraph to make sure you understand before going on.

2. But let's say the new information does not match up with anything in your memory. Your brain then continues to process by executing step two. Step two is actually a decision the brain must make to take one of two alternative routes:

A. It seeks additional information. It tries to answer the question, What is "Brensello's"? A brand of ice cream? A shoe? A hardware store? The name of a street? What is "Brensello's"?

If your brain decides to take this route, it must actively go on an information-gathering expedition. It must now kick the word "Brensello's" up to the conscious level of attention and deal with it there. Once this happens, everything slows down considerably. Instant impact can be made only subconsciously. Once the brain decides to deal with your information on the conscious level, your opportunity to make an instant impact is gone. Am I saying it's undesirable to make conscious impressions, that it's not good to have people become consciously aware of your message? No. Conscious impressions are valuable, but they're much more difficult to create. Consequently, they happen much less frequently than subconscious impressions.

At any rate, your brain now directs you to take specific information-gathering behavior, such as to ask the person riding in the car with you what "Brensello's" is, or to look intently at the building on which the "Brensello's" sign is attached to see what it looks like. Or it directs you to any other type of activity that would possibly give it the information it needs to assign the word "Brensello's" a meaning. Since this route requires conscious attention and behavior and requires considerably more brain power, it seldom happens. Usually the brain will opt for route B.*

B. Your brain rejects the information. It cannot produce a match between the newly-sighted word "Brensello's" and anything similar in storage, and it doesn't feel like bothering the conscious mind with the trivial task of finding the meaning (remember, the brain likes to avoid work if it can). So it decides not to deal with the word. To continue to search for meaning by seeking additional information is just not worth the trouble. So the word "Brensello's" is thrown out. Rejected. Turned away at the gate. This sighting of the word "Brensello's" has made no impact.

Most of the time, the brain will opt for route B, since it's the route of least resistance. That's why most of the time information reaching the brain gets rejected.

HOW INSTANT IMPACT HAPPENS

Are you still with me? This discussion may seem quite microscopic and detailed, but sharp marketers who aspire to rise above the others will need to know this material. Hang with me and you'll be well rewarded.

What do you want a person's brain to do when it sees your logo or hears your company name? Certainly you don't want the brain to reject it. Nor do you want the brain to have to make a conscious effort to seek a meaning, since doing so has many disadvantages.

---

*Route A actually involves two other functions, *categorization* and *evaluation*. Your brain must assign a category to the information as a way of keeping it organized along with every other piece of information. Evaluation involves assigning a relative value to the information, based on whether the information is good or bad for you. I won't go into greater detail about categorization and evaluation, since a deeper understanding of them is not necessary. Simply realize that Route A processing is a rather complex, time-consuming procedure.

First of all, it takes longer. And the longer it takes, the weaker the impact. Second, the brain may assign an inaccurate meaning to your logo, or a meaning that carries a negative evaluation. This happens all the time, when additional information about you comes from one of your competitors. When the brain resorts to this level of processing, it does so at the marketer's risk. This alternative is not desirable either.

The best alternative we've seen yet occurs when the brain successfully matches a piece of newly-received information with previously-received information in memory. When this happens, the new information is assigned a meaning and is immediately routed to that part of the brain that accepts impressions. Therefore, *when your logo or name matches something in a person's memory, it has made a strong subconscious impression, in an instant's time.*

So how do you, the marketer, cause this to happen? How do you make sure your logo matches up with the correct meaning in people's brains? Must a person be familiar with your logo or name before this can happen? If so, a brand new product or service is handicapped by its unfamiliar nature. And what if your product or service has been around for a while, yet most of your logo sightings have been rejected by people's brains? You could spend a ton of money on additional logo exposures, but those too might be rejected because they still don't match with anything in memory.

How would you feel if you knew that each and every time people saw your logo or heard your name, a processing match occurred in their brains, and your logo or name made an instant, strong impression? Would that improve your overall impact by a significant degree? You'd better believe it would! It wouldn't take long for demand to rise and sales results to show, either.

MAKE INSTANT IMPACT BY PRE-PROCESSING

The secret lies in a technique called *pre-processing*. When you pre-process, you avert the brain's processing function altogether by providing the brain with a meaning to go along with your name or logo. In other words, the brain *receives your logo and a meaning at the same time,* thus negating its need to process your logo. Pre-processing results in an even stronger and quicker impression than when the brain processes and matches! And it happens *every time* the brain receives your logo or name!

You pre-process by providing the brain with a piece of information—a special word—that it is already familiar with and attaching your name or logo to it. We call this special word a *pre-processed word,* since the brain is already familiar with it.

When you pre-process, you are doing for the mind what Gatorade does for the body. The body converts sugar into glucose, which it then uses for energy. Gatorade contains glucose, which is pre-processed sugar. When the body receives Gatorade, it does not need to process sugar into glucose, for glucose has already been received. Instant energy results.

Pre-Processing Examples

The best example of pre-processing actually occurred a few decades ago. Remember when Coca-Cola used to have the word "Drink" in front of their logo? It was practically part of their logo. Wherever the Coca-Cola logo appeared, the word "Drink" appeared before it (positioned to the left or above). "Drink" is a great pre-processed word. Not only does everyone know what it means, but also it can be both a verb and a noun, as in "Hold the bottle up to your mouth and drink Coca-Cola" (drink used as a verb), and "Drink: Coca-Cola," meaning Coca-Cola is a drink (noun version).

Another example also goes back a few decades. Remember driving through the country and passing diner after diner that had the word "EAT" in huge letters above their names? "Eat" is another great pre-processed word. Everyone knows what it is and everyone can relate to it at least three times a day.

We advise our radio station clients to attach the word "Radio" or "Listen" to the front of their logos. Likewise, we advise our television station clients to place either "Television" or "Watch" in front of their logos. Remember, the brain needs to know what your logo means or it'll start processing. It may not know what "K-93" is without the word "radio" attached. (Once a logo has

FIGURE 1
Examples of pre-processed logos (fictitious brands).

been in use in a particular market or trading area for at least eight years, the pre-processed word can be changed from a noun to a verb. Thus a station could go from "Radio" to "Listen".)

Look at Figure 1. It contains a few examples of logos (for fictitious products) with pre-processed words attached.

THE KEY TO PRE-PROCESSING'S EFFECTIVENESS

I know what you're thinking. "A pre-processed word may help a new product or service gain familiarity, but everyone already knows what my product is," you point out.

There are two problems with that reasoning. First, despite what you may believe, fewer people know what your name means than you think, especially if you've been in a particular market or trading area for less than eight years. There still may be a large number of people who either have never heard of you or have an erroneous impression of you. A radio ratings survey once revealed that some people thought "K-93" was a new bug spray. Others thought it was an automotive lubricant. The radio station brass had to be scraped off the floor. It had never occurred to them someone might not know what "K-93" was.

Second, telling people what your name or logo means is only part of what you accomplish through pre-processing. At the beginning of this chapter I talked about gaining top-of-mind awareness in a relatively short period of time. This is a by-product of pre-processing that is as equally important as making an instant impression. Herein lies the real key to the effectiveness of pre-processing. By providing a pre-processed word and attaching your name or logo to it, *you are programming the receiver's brain to store the two—the pre-processed word and name or logo—together as one piece of information.* When that occurs, your name automatically pops into a person's consciousness when the pre-processed word first flashes in the mind.

Here's how it works: A person gets thirsty. Her brain signals that it wants to drink. This can happen either subconsciously or consciously. The latter often happening in the company of another person when one verbally expresses the desire to the other ("I'd like a drink" or "Let's get something to drink"). The word "Drink" is the trigger word that causes the attached product name to shoot up into consciousness. That's why even the world's most recognizable logo, Coca-Cola, would still benefit by attaching itself to the pre-processed word "Drink".

When a radio ratings company asks a survey respondent what radio station they listen to, what set of call letters or moniker comes to mind first? Since the trigger word "radio" (or "listen") is mentioned in the question "What radio station do you listen to?", the radio station which attached its logo to the pre-processed word "radio" (or "listen") and made numerous impressions as such will be recalled first.

By pre-processing, not only are you averting the brain's processing system, but also you're programming the brain to recall your name instantly when prompted. You can see why pre-processing is such a powerful and important technique to adopt.

HOW TO PRE-PROCESS

- **Step 1. Choose a pre-processed word.** If your product or service has been on the market for fewer than eight years, your pre-processed word must be descriptive. A noun is recommended. It must provide receivers with information that allows them to categorize you. If your product or service has been in a particular trading area for over eight years, consider switching to a verb.

  For example, the pre-processed word "Restaurant" or "Food" tells someone what you are. The word "Eat" implies you're either a restaurant or a food, which is not quite so good as coming right out and stating what you are. But "Eat" has an off-setting advantage in that it is more likely to come up in conversation (whether the brain is talking to itself, or two or more people are conversing). Also, "Eat" is a more bottom-line motive; people need to eat. The word "Hungry" would also work well for a restaurant or food item that has been around for over eight years.

- **Step 2. Link your brand name (in spoken or logo form) with your pre-processed word.** It's better to position your pre-processed word before your logo (to the left or above) rather than after (to the right or below). Remember, your pre-processed word comes to mind first, and your name rides on its coattails, such as when your friend gets you past the gate by telling the guard, "He's with me."

  Look at Figure 1, on page 113, once again. The pre-processed word "Fun!" is positioned above the name "Brad's." After a number of impressions are made on a person's subconscious, what will pop into that person's mind when he thinks of having some fun? More than likely, the name Brad's.

  The attachment of a pre-processed word with a name or logo should be fairly permanent. In fact, if you design your logo to include your pre-processed word, the two become one, which is what you're trying to make happen in the receiver's brain anyway.

ADVANCED PRE-PROCESSING

The ultimate in pre-processing occurs when your brand name and pre-processing word are one and the same. How is that achieved? Consider these examples:

Take the name "Wonder Bread". The brand name is really the word "Wonder" (which carries a positive connotation, by the way, since it implies power or amazement), and the word "Bread" is the pre-processed word, or component. You put the two together and create a product name with built-in pre-processing.

Same with Minute Rice, Fast Frame, and Jiffy Lube.

How about Tire America, Computerland, Pizza Hut, and Food Lion? The words "Tire," "Computer," "Pizza," and "Food" are the pre-processed components. These names are even stronger than Wonder Bread, Minute Rice, Fast Frame, and Jiffy Lube because the pre-processed word, or component in this case, is first in sequence.

CAUTION AHEAD

There are two important ideas you must adopt, or you're going to have a difficult time with pre-processing.

First, do not let the seeming awkwardness of pre-processing bother you. Having a pre-processed word attached to the front end of your logo may seem pretty strange; it may seem out of place or illogical. But the public isn't aware of any awkwardness. People are not consciously analyzing your logo as you are. And it seems awkward to you only because you're not used to it. After a few years, your feelings of awkwardness will reverse, and it would really seem awkward if you removed your pre-processed word from your logo.

Second, you must keep in mind that all pre-processing happens subconsciously. The impressions you make are all received subconsciously, and the recall of your name happens subconsciously. A person doesn't know why the name Brad's suddenly comes to mind when he thinks of doing something that's fun, he just knows it does.

Many marketers overrate the value of making conscious impressions and underrate the value of making subconscious impressions. That's why you see so many "teaser" campaigns on billboards. Marketers want to raise their billboards to the conscious level of attention. They want to "create talk" by getting people to wonder what the billboard is all about. This is the exact opposite of pre-processing. It not only causes the brain to process, it also makes it *difficult* for the brain to find a meaning. How many times do you think such a billboard is rejected by the brain? My estimate is that 999 out of 1,000 sightings result in rejection, and no impact.

On the other hand, if you pre-process your billboards by showing little more than your pre-processed word and logo, big and bold, how many instant subconscious impressions will you make? How about 1,000 impressions out of 1,000 sightings? Of course, you may not "create talk" with such a board, but so what? If no one is talking about your billboard, you know it's working. If people are talking about it, you know it is time to re-design it for stronger subconscious impact.

Let me repeat a point I made earlier. Conscious impressions are fine, they work. But if you care only about making impressions on the conscious level, your advertising as a whole will be very weak and very inefficient. Pre-processing makes impressions on the subconscious level. Subconscious impressions are much easier to do, much more efficient, and much more productive.

Chapter Eleven

Attract New Customers by Widening Your Appeal

One of the greatest ways to start and build demand is to widen the appeal range of your product or service. Doing so can result in a rather dramatic leap in demand within a short period of time. Unfortunately, for every one marketer that understands how to go about widening appeal properly, nine other marketers either misunderstand the process and botch it up or don't even believe in widening appeal at all and thus never attempt it. Nine out of ten marketers, therefore, suffer from self-inflicted demand limitation. If you want to be the one out of ten that rises above, you'll get a lot out of this chapter.

Widening the appeal of a product or service is really a function of targeting. Since even the simplest discussion of targeting can get confusing, we're going to look at the targeting process in a way that makes it easy to understand and discuss. This way of looking at things may be quite different from what you're used to, and may use terminology in different ways from what you're used to, so let's start by establishing a common understanding.

THE CORE AND FRINGE

For almost every type of product or service in existence, there also exists a number of consumers who are heavy users of same. Heavy users buy and use the type of product or service often. They are collectively referred to as *core* consumers and are defined mainly using standard demographic measures (the psychographic dimension will be addressed in Chapter 16). For example, core beer drinkers are males between 18 and 44 years of age. Core buyers of tennis shoes are males and females between the ages of 16 and 28 who reside in middle income or higher households and who play tennis regularly.

The core is a thin segment of the total population, a small slice of the pie. When your marketing is designed to reach and affect only the core, as when a tennis shoe marketer crafts ads and buys media to hit middle income-plus people between the ages of 16 and 28 who play tennis, you're said to be "targeting your core."

People who buy and use a product or service in smaller quantity or with less frequency than the core are called *fringe* consumers. Demographically speaking, the fringe falls outside of your tightly defined core. For the tennis shoe marketer, the fringe may be people under 16 and over 28 who play tennis irregularly or not at all. When you design your marketing to appeal to people outside of your core, you're said to be "targeting your fringe." When you design your marketing to appeal to your fringe as well as your core, you're said to be "targeting your core and fringe."

Core and fringe consumers together compose 100 percent of the potential buying population for your type of product or service. If a person has never or is unlikely ever to buy your type of product, that person falls out of your buying population and is contained in neither the core nor fringe category for your product type.

CORE TARGETING IS NOT THE NAME OF THE GAME

Hardly a week goes by without some marketing or advertising executive reiterating the popular belief that "pinpointing" consumers and "zeroing in" with thinly targeted marketing is the name of the game. Some marketers consider themselves all the wiser as they devise an ever-increasing number of ways to avoid mass marketing and "micro market" or "niche market" only to a thin slice of the entire consumer pie.

Simple logic would seem to agree. After all, if you're a marketer of athletic shoes, you ought to market to athletes. That's how the athletic shoe industry began...shoes made for and marketed to athletes. But some of the big-selling brands of the 50s, 60s, and 70s, such as Converse, U.S. Keds, P. F. Flyer and Adidas, never looked beyond the sports-oriented, heavy user core. These companies still sell athletic shoes, but only to core consumers. (Of the three, Keds recently began looking beyond their core and has experienced an upward turn in sales.)

Then along came Nike, Reebok, and L.A. Gear in the 80s and 90s. They didn't follow simple logic. They began marketing to the fringe as well as the core; they designed their marketing to reach and appeal to the light user as well as the heavy user. The result? Sales exploded, and Nike, Reebok, and L.A. Gear left the core-oriented brands behind in the dust. The next time you see someone wearing an athletic shoe while engaging in some non-athletic activity, such as shopping, running errands, or just lounging around the house, the chances are he or she will be wearing a Nike, Reebok, or L.A. Gear shoe as opposed to any other brand.

I always get a chuckle when I hear someone trumpeting the advantages of the ever-increasing media "fragmentation," as though greater fragmentation, when each media outlet delivers a thinner slice of the pie, is good for the marketer. The media are becoming increasingly fragmented because there are an ever-increasing number of media outlets in existence, forcing each one to end up with a thinner slice of the audience pie. Media fragmentation did not come about because the media decided to do the marketer a favor. If anything, fragmentation makes things more difficult for the marketer, as she must now buy more media outlets to reach the same number of consumers she previously reached with fewer outlets.

Of course, the marketer could do the opposite. He could "take advantage" of the fragmentation and buy fewer media outlets altogether. By selecting the "right" outlets, based on the types of consumers they "deliver," he can not only "zero in" on his core consumer more easily, but also he can save money in the process by eliminating the "waste," that is, the fringe.

Or so he thinks. Read on to learn how things really work.

The Disadvantages of Targeting Thinly

When you target your marketing to reach and affect only your core, you're likely to experience three hefty problems.

First, there's a strong chance you're limiting your sales significantly. A lot more potential sales exist beyond your thinly defined core than you may think. Besides, your goal is to create major demand... that's why you're reading this book. If you limit yourself to core-targeted marketing only, you lessen your chances of achieving that goal.

Second, you forfeit the opportunity to enlarge your core. Core enlargement is accomplished by converting light users into heavy users. The only way to do that is to direct some of your marketing toward your fringe and persuade them accordingly.

Third, core-targeted marketing can quickly result in wasted media expenditures. Most marketers think it's the other way around, that targeting beyond their core results in greater waste. Not so. Contrary to conventional belief, *the waste of media expenditures becomes much more severe when you target thinly and zero in than when you target widely and spread it out.* I'll explain exactly how this happens in a minute. For now, follow along as we explore further.

The Core Obsession Trap

When marketers become obsessed with their core, when they believe the key to success is to super-serve the core at the expense of the fringe, they fall into the Core Obsession Trap. These people design their entire marketing program and make all subsequent decisions based on one primary directive: Target the core.

As a consultant, I see marketers falling into this trap quite often. I'm sure you've seen it as well. The most noticeable symptom of a trapped marketer is that he rejects every marketing tactic that doesn't directly target his core. If it's not core-targeted, he doesn't do it.

Believe it or not, some marketers actually are obsessed with the core of the core! They target so thinly they need a microscope to see what it is they're doing. A radio station program director once mentioned that their core was a 24-year-old single female who works during the day and goes dancing at night. Sometimes talking about your core in such definitive terms can be helpful; it can keep you focused. But when you reject every marketing tactic that reaches beyond this core-of-the-core bullseye and spend all your time and money trying to hit it with every punch you throw, you're dangerously obsessed.

Core obsession results in significantly less demand and a greater waste of the media budget. Yet many marketers mistakenly believe the opposite, that the key to building demand and spending wisely is to target exclusively to their core. Why do these marketers fall victim to the Core Obsession Trap? There are three main reasons.

First of all, marketers can end up disproportionately serving their core by over-responding to the desires of their core. Chances are the people that give you feedback, the active consumers that take the time to tell you what they think of your product, will come from the core category. In other words, your core will contain the most vocal consumers. You'll hear from them and you'll be well aware of their needs and desires. When you respond to these people in a big way and begin crafting your product and your marketing to satisfy them exclusively, you risk alienating your fringe. Your fringe has somewhat different desires from your core. Yet you may seldom hear from fringe consumers, and you may not even know who they are. Don't assume that the people you hear from, your core, represent the preferences of all consumers. They don't.

Second, marketers sometimes willfully design their marketing to super-serve their core because they misunderstand the old 80/20 Rule. The 80/20 Rule is not really a rule at all, but simply a recognition of the tendency for 80 percent of your sales to come from 20 percent of your customers. The 80/20 Rule may apply to personal selling—you wouldn't want your sales force spending the majority of their time with the customers that generate the least revenue—but it has nothing to do with marketing. Marketing, after all, recruits new customers and determines to a large degree which of them become your big spenders today and in the future.

Third, some marketers mistakenly believe it's inefficient, or not cost-effective, to market beyond their core. They believe that if one markets outside of one's core, one is blowing the budget on "wasted exposure." "Why reach a lot of people that are not the primary users of my type of product?", they reason. "I'd rather increase market share by targeting core consumers than try to convince the less inclined to give us a try."

Here's the fallacy of that reasoning. The natural forces of the marketplace dictate that *you're going to get only so much market share from your core no matter what you do or how long you keep doing it*. Once you reach this point, called the *core maximization level*, the marketing money you allocate to increase core market share becomes terribly inefficient.

This is a fact of reality many marketers refuse to acknowledge. They fail to realize that there is a practical limit to the amount of core market share they can prudently attain. They fail to understand that it can cost a great deal more to boost market share in the core category than it can cost to generate an equal increase in revenue from a boost in fringe market share. Consequently, they end up spending thousands upon thousands, or millions upon millions, of dollars trying to suck every quarter point of market share out of their core. Like wretchedly squeezing every last drop of juice out of a spent grapefruit. If a core-obsessed marketer actually calculated how much it cost to gain every fractional point of market share beyond the core maximization level, he'd require electro-shock treatment to live another day.

But marketers caught in the Core Obsession Trap never believe they have reached the core maximization level. They believe there is no practical limit to the amount of core market share they can acquire. So they keep throwing more and more money at their core, much like obsessed gamblers who never think they've reached their limit, believing the next roll will be the big winner. Both gamblers and core obsessors keep investing, but keep getting less and less return for each incremental dollar.

Did you ever spend a good chunk of your marketing budget only to realize little, if any, significant sales increase? Could it be you were targeting a depleted core? When you reach your core maximization level, you must look to the fringe for growth. Remember, the fringe may be just as likely to purchase your product or service as the core if they have some motivation. You may be surprised how relatively easy it is to increase overall market share when you stop concentrating on the core exclusively and pay a little attention to the fringe.

FRINGE TARGETING IS INEVITABLE

I've got news for you. You're going to end up targeting your fringe anyway, whether you like the idea or not. Why? Because of almighty growth. As you know, growth is the master we all serve in the business world. If your revenues aren't growing year after year (or quarter after quarter in some circles), you're a dead company. How do you keep revenues growing quarter after quarter, year after year? Once you hit the core maximization level, all future growth comes from your fringe.

Look at what's happening in the financial services industry. Banks are targeting well beyond their core by providing stock brokerage services as well as standard banking services. And stock brokerages are offering money market accounts with check-writing privileges. So we have banks acting like brokerages and brokerages acting like banks. Why? They've reached their respective core maximization levels and they've got to find other ways of attracting fringe consumers in order to grow.

Fast food marketers are expanding their menus like crazy, trying to attract fringe consumers. Marketers of sound equipment are starting to target females, who are outside of their dominantly male core. Suntan lotions are starting to target males, who are outside of their dominantly female core. I just heard an Office America radio commercial this morning touting their supply of household furnishings.

Politicians know that if they do not target beyond their core group of supporters, they'll never win an election. It's the fringe voters, the people that don't have strong feelings one way or the other, that politicians must win to put them over the top on election day.

Why do you think so many top marketers buy television time during the Super Bowl every year, at astronomical prices? The Super Bowl draws such a wide-ranging audience they can reach a whole lot of fringe (as well as core) consumers with one commercial. Mass marketing is not dead. It's alive and thriving under the blanket of media fragmentation.

What if your product or service is specifically designed to appeal to a small market niche? It wouldn't make sense to mass market a niche product, would it? Not if you can remain happy operating within the confines of your chosen niche. But a funny thing happens to many marketers of niche products. They become unhappy when sales level off after a few short years. They become very unhappy when they subsequently spend lots and lots of money trying to boost sales by targeting their niche . . . and sales barely uptick as a result. Once you reach your core maximization level, you have a choice. Either be satisfied with slow or no growth (not an altogether unwise choice, as long as you don't have stockholders or lenders leaning on you), or begin marketing to your fringe for more substantial growth.

THE OPTIMUM STRATEGY

Serve both your core and fringe, but neither to such an extreme you ignore the other. It's as simple as that.

There is an exception. When you first launch a new product or service, your optimum strategy is to target the core consumer exclusively. Like piercing the skin with a sharp needle rather than with a blunt object, you can enter a market much easier by starting with a thinly targeted, highly focused effort. Once you gain entry and begin picking up market share from the core, however, you should begin focusing some attention on the fringe. By the time you reach your core maximization level, you should be focusing a great deal on your fringe.

For example, Domino's Pizza spent the first few years of its existence targeting strictly its heavy-user core. This happened to be college students at Eastern Michigan University, the University of Michigan, and, later, Michigan State University. But once they reached their core maximization level—once these college kids were gobbling as much pizza as they were ever going to—Domino's began targeting their fringe and marketing to people other than college students.

Of course, the possibility of going to the opposite extreme from the Core Obsession Trap exists. Sometimes marketers abandon their core entirely in an effort to gain fringe patronization. They consequently lose focus and appear confused. Core patronization starts to erode. And once core erosion sets in, it's hard to stop. Here's an example. By definition, the core for CHR radio stations is males and females 18 to 34. Everything else is fringe. But some CHR stations are trying to become more "adult" in nature and are thus targeting more and more to their 35–49 fringe. Targeting to the 35–49 fringe is okay, as long as it augments some strong 18–34 targeting. But when these so-called "adult CHRs" go too far and start abandoning their core, guess what happens? The ratings drop and they can't figure out why. Moral: Always pay attention to your core. Just don't super-serve it to the detriment of the fringe.

CORE AND FRINGE TENDENCIES

The first step in learning how to work your core and fringe for maximum demand is to take notice of some key tendencies.

- **The size of your core and fringe depends on your product.** By definition, your core has tight demographic parameters. Your fringe, by definition, has wide demographic parameters. But neither definition says anything about the relative size of each, based on the number of people that may fall into each category.

  If you're marketing an esoteric, high ticket item, such as a super high quality, $1,200 tone arm for turntables, your core is going to be virtually 100 percent of your consumers. Your fringe will be almost nonexistent because no one outside of your core, which is well-off audiophile males between 30 and 45, is likely ever to buy your product.

If you're marketing a nonesoteric, nonhigh ticket item, such as athletic shoes, your fringe will be much larger than your core. Observe: The number of people between 14 and 28 who buy and wear athletic shoes often for regular sporting activity—the core—is far fewer than the total number of people of all other ages who engage in light (or no) sporting activity, yet buy and wear the shoes nonetheless.

- **A person is a fringe or core consumer depending on item.** There is no such thing as a "core person" or a "fringe person" all the time. A person may be either, and may switch categories, depending on the product or service in question. For example, a person may be a core consumer of designer suits and a fringe consumer of lawn care equipment, or vice versa.

- **Fringe consumers are just as susceptible to influence as core consumers.** Your fringe consumers may have a lower level of interest in your product or service than your core consumers and may buy less frequently, but they do buy and are affected by good marketing. In fact, fringe consumers are often more susceptible to your marketing than core consumers, since core consumers will often formulate opinions based on other nonadvertised information they dig up.

- **Core and fringe consumers have different needs and desires and respond to different marketing stimuli.** In many cases, core consumers of a particular product or service display a high degree of interest in and enthusiasm for the product or service. They're "into it." They salivate over detailed information. They are curious about how it's made, or where it comes from. They like to talk about it. They may even congregate with other core consumers with similar interest.

  The fringe, on the other hand, wants bottom-line information and wants it quickly. The fringe needs to know simply that your product exists and what it does. The fringe also thrives on convenience. The quicker and easier it is and the less thought necessary to make the purchase and take possession, the more they'll buy. A fringe consumer doesn't spend much time talking about the product or service, he just buys it and mentally moves on.

HOW TO ATTRACT NEW CUSTOMERS
BY WIDENING YOUR APPEAL

Widening appeal is nothing more than marketing beyond your core. You should be able to implement these procedures without much difficulty.

- **Step 1. Identify the needs and desires of your core.** To find out whether your core prefers green tennis shoes with thin laces or red tennis shoes with fat laces, simply ask them. Include a questionnaire in every box. Or call them to ask how the product is working out and to solicit their comments. Remember, the core generally likes to talk about the product or service. It doesn't take much prompting to get them to tell you all you need to know (they'll probably tell you more than you care to hear).

- **Step 2. Identify the needs and desires of your fringe.** Soliciting detailed information from your fringe is not nearly so easy as it is from your core. The fringe, you'll recall, has a lower level of interest and won't spend the time or energy talking about it. This is one reason marketing research fails so often. A randomly selected sample of consumers can turn out to include a disproportionately heavy dose of core consumers. The core consumer is more likely to step forward and respond to surveys about the product or service in question, whereas the fringe consumer elects not to bother with it. There is one simple way to ascertain detailed fringe preferences. Observe. It doesn't take much. Observe a few casual consumers in action.

Did you know the entire CHR radio format (called Top 40 at the time of its inception), characterized by the playing of the top-charting songs over and over again, was born of the simple observation that people in a restaurant tend to play the same few songs over and over again on the juke box?

Athletic shoe marketers observed nonathletes buying the shoes for everyday wear, the majority of whom did nothing more than casual walking in them. So they began marketing to this fringe segment. L.A. Gear took it one step further and coined the term "street hiking." They made a line of shoes specifically for "street hikers" and created a whole ad campaign designed to reach and appeal to them.

Arm & Hammer Baking Soda noticed people using the product for a lot of other things besides baking. So they began marketing to the fringe users—the people who don't bake things—by telling them about all the other things they can do with the product, including absorbing refrigerator odors and soothing their upset stomachs.

- **Step 3. Cater to both your core and fringe in terms of message.** Create some ads and promotions that speak both to the core and to the fringe. It's usually easier to create separate ads for each category of consumer, rather than to appeal to both categories in each single ad.

- **Step 4. Cater to both your core and fringe in terms of media selection.** Buy highly targeted media for your core ads and mass appeal media for your fringe ads.

- **Step 5. Use the Sprinkler Strategy.** A rotating water sprinkler wets the entire lawn by spraying water in only one direction at a time, but constantly changing direction at the same time. You can do the same with your advertising and promotions. Shoot some ads in the direction of your core. Then pivot and do a fringe promotion. Then pivot and shoot some ads in the direction of your fringe. Then pivot again and do a core promotion. Keep pivoting and keep mixing it up. You can overlap many selected ad runs and/or promotions, or run some simultaneously. This is not meant to sound like a haphazard or unplanned approach. The Sprinkler Strategy is a well-planned, well-orchestrated campaign. It keeps you attentive to the various needs of your core and fringe elements. If you constantly pivot, and don't ignore one element long enough for it to get "dry," you'll maximize impact and be well on your way to creating massive demand!

Chapter Twelve

Direct Mail Deployment

M any demand-creating techniques are implemented through advertising in various media outlet types, such as radio, television, magazines, newspapers, billboards, etc. As you've noticed, I've been explaining how to implement in these media outlet types as we've been going along. But there's one media outlet that warrants its own chapter.

Because of the unique attributes of direct mail, it is very conducive to many of our demand-creating techniques. Also, it's becoming very popular with many marketers that have their own databases going. Unfortunately, direct mail is often misunderstood and misused. You need to be able to take full advantage of direct mail, and you need to reduce your chances of misusing it. You will accomplish both with this chapter.

DIRECT MAIL MISCONCEPTIONS

First let's clear up some popular myths about direct mail advertising.

- **Myth: It's junk mail—people don't read it.**
  Truth: People read their mail. I guarantee, if I sent you a

letter, you'd open it and read it. And it's the same if you sent me one. "But you're talking about a personal letter," you say. "What about a printed advertising piece?"

The only reasons a person does not open and read an advertising piece are that (a) they already know what it contains, and (b) they already know they're not interested. But how does a person come to these two conclusions? They notice the outside of the piece and judge accordingly. If your piece is properly designed, it will make an impression, even if it subsequently goes straight into the trash. Direct mail advertising pieces make no less an impression than billboards or magazine ads, in most cases. Said another way, if a person looks at the outside of your piece, then elects to throw it out, it's done its job. Any further impact, which does occur quite often, is bonus or residual impact.

By and large, people enjoy receiving mail (except for bills, perhaps). For every one person who complains about being on some mailing list, five other people sign up to receive product or service information in their mail. Receiving mail is a delightful experience. Want proof? Watch how quickly people fetch their mail after it arrives. When people come home from work, what's one of the first things they like to do?

The term junk mail really doesn't refer to pieces that make an impression and then get trashed. The majority of *all* advertising, direct mail included, is physically or mentally trashed right after the impression (you don't see many people cutting couponless ads from magazines or newspapers and saving them, nor do many people tape-record radio and television commercials for later review). Trashed advertising comes with the territory, no matter what media outlet types you use.

Junk mail does apply to a poorly conceived, poorly written, poorly designed piece, or a piece promoting a poor quality product or some scam. (The preferred technical term for such among marketing professionals is "piece of crap.") When you mail out pieces of crap, the myth of people not reading them will become the reality.

- **Myth: People don't respond to direct mail.**
Truth: People respond exceptionally well to direct mail. People fill out, return, clip, save, sniff, call 800 numbers . . . whatever. Direct mail is an aggressive, intrusive advertising vehicle. It can motivate people to act and to act quickly.

  Direct mail, like all advertising, is subject to "the numbers." The more pieces you mail out, the more response you'll get. But it's also subject to a number of seemingly inconsequential details which turn out to be anything but inconsequential in affecting response rate. Later in this chapter, I'll offer four tips that you can use to ensure a decent response each and every time you mail.

- **Myth: Direct mail is very expensive.**
Truth: All advertising media are expensive. However, like all other media, there are ways to do direct mail economically. A small retailer can direct mail to 10,000 households in the immediate trading area for only a few hundred dollars with a "shared" mailer such as Val Pak. ("Shared" means the costs of the mailing are divided among the many businesses whose pieces are all contained in the envelope or booklet mailed.) Compared with most other advertising vehicles, we're talking dirt cheap here. Yet the response can be very good.

  Even a full color self-mailer can be done very reasonably. Your per-piece printing cost drops significantly if you mail over 100,000 pieces or so. Additional savings occur if your mailing labels are carrier route pre-sorted, and if you mail to at least 90 percent of all addresses in each Zip Code.

  You can also hit your core consumers or customers relatively inexpensively when you maintain an in-house database. More on this later.

THE ADVANTAGES OF DIRECT MAIL

Direct mail is very conducive to implementing many of our demand-creating techniques. Here's what you can accomplish with direct mail:

- **Interact with your core.** Direct mail can be targeted precisely to the people you desire. It's great for working your core. Remember, the core likes detailed information and likes to receive communication from you.

- **Reach your fringe.** The fringe is, by nature, rather elusive. The fringe may not step forward to initiate communication with you, but you can step forward and communicate with them. Not everyone reads the publications, watches the television shows, or drives by the billboards you advertise in. But everyone must live somewhere, and that somewhere has an address. Direct mail reaches into the depths of your market and hits people you never knew existed but who will buy nonetheless.

- **Persuade in detail.** The written word can be very commanding. While long copy is often undesirable in newspaper and magazine ads, it often works well in direct mail pieces.

- **Support your other media outlet types.** The CBS television network uses its own airtime to promote upcoming shows and advertises in *TV Guide* and selected newspapers. But did you know they also direct mail to various types of people who may have a special interest in a particular show? One "48 Hours" show, for example, dealt with the advertising industry, so CBS bought a mailing list of advertising people and shot out notices.

- **Mobilize people.** Did you ever try to buy tickets to a Grateful Dead concert? By the time word gets out they're coming to town—even by the time the media first hear about it—the concert is already sold out! How does that happen? The Dead maintains a database of hundreds of thousands of people and mails to them regularly, keeping them apprised of each upcoming concert and selling them tickets well in advance.

  A radio station sold a remote broadcast to a car dealer client of theirs, convincing the dealer the Saturday afternoon remote would draw a large crowd. Unbeknown to the dealer, the station direct mailed to a few thousand people in their database that lived near the dealership about a week before the scheduled remote. (The mail piece itself was a letter from the station's program director informing people about the upcoming remote broadcast, including mention of the T-shirts and music cassettes to be given away, and asking them to attend.) The station thus increased their chances of getting a good turnout even before the promotional mentions aired. In this instance, the remote ended up drawing a "record-breaking crowd," aided in part by the direct mail piece.

- **Expose without display.** When you purchase exposure in most media outlet types—radio, television, newspaper, magazine, billboard, etc.—your ads are on display for anyone and everyone to see. That, of course, is what you want. Or perhaps naked display is not exactly what you want. There may be times when you prefer that your competitors and all the world *not* see what you're marketing quite yet. In a later chapter you're going to see that there are times when you do not want certain types of people to see your advertising. You still, however, want to achieve the kind of high impact exposure that a mass medium provides. Direct mail is your answer. That's why many marketers call direct mail their "secret weapon."

- **Make multiple impact.** One single direct mail piece can produce benefits which ripple on and on.

  First, you achieve *frontal impact* when your pieces first hit mailboxes and make their initial impression on the recipients.

  Second, you achieve *participating impact* as people see your piece many times during the period in which your piece is "alive" or "active." I'm referring mainly to pieces designed around a contest that keeps people playing for a number of weeks. Or pieces that contain multiple coupons with staggered and consecutive validation dates. Or pieces that contain a month-long calendar of events. Or pieces that contain reference information.

  Third, you get *residual impact* when people respond. Response may be in the form of a contest entry card or a product order blank the recipient has filled out and sent back.

Or an order the recipient may call in via telephone. Or the redemption of a coupon when the recipient physically trots into your store.

THE DUAL MAILING STRATEGY

You really should have two separate mailing programs in effect.

Program One: Do regular mailings to your core. Core-directed mailings should be done regularly, such as once per month or once per quarter. These are just a routine part of core maintenance.

Luckily, we live in a time when inexpensive computers and excellent database programs are readily available. You should set up and maintain an in-house database if you haven't already done so. Build your database by collecting names and addresses of customers who return recycle cards (explained in the next chapter), warranty registration cards, contest activator or entry cards, or product order blanks.

Core mailings are not strictly dependent upon an in-house database. Core mailings can be done with a purchased mail list as well. List companies offer lists broken down by sex, age, occupation, and a whole host of other variables.

Program Two: Once or twice per year do a major, high-profile, high-impact mailing to both your core and fringe together. This is like net fishing. Your huge net sweeps the marketplace and rakes in all kinds of living organisms—most of whom have never dealt with you before. The purpose is to recruit new customers and to inspire people who are not currently buying your product or service to sample you. You will find that a well-conceived, well-executed direct mail campaign is an excellent customer recruitment tool.

To do an effective core+fringe mailing, you must purchase a mailing list from a list company. Your own database will not do, since the object is to reach people who are not currently buying your product or service or may never even have heard of you (although you may augment with your database list).

"WHAT DO I MAIL?"

A client radio station once spent several weeks setting up a database system and entering the names and addresses of old contest entrants. After they'd entered over 7,000 names and were ready to print their first batch of labels, it suddenly occurred to them they had no idea what they should mail to these people. A letter of some sort? A newsletter? A contest piece? What?

Since summer was approaching and a number of their air personalities would soon be taking vacations, I jokingly suggested the station mail postcards from exotic locations signed by the jocks. I then offered my real suggestions, which were not quite so flamboyant. On my next visit a few months later, the general manager couldn't wait to show me what they'd mailed. She handed me a postcard...but not just any postcard. One side was a full color photo of the morning jock pulling some kind of fish out of the water, with him and the fish grinning from ear to ear (or fin to fin). The reverse side had a handwritten note asking people to "keep listenin' while I'm fishin'." The postcard was a big hit, both in the company (which has since used the idea at its other stations) and with the public.

What you mail is limited only by your imagination. However, there are some key ingredients that an effective direct mail piece should contain.

For Regular, Core-Directed Mailings

Your piece can take any shape or size that you like. But make sure it contains some or all of these ingredients:

- **A "personal" letter or note.** Make it from someone in charge ...the owner, president, or manager.
- **A coupon.** Coupons are, and will continue to be, a valuable part of marketing. When you issue a coupon worth $1 off, you've just handed the recipient a $1 bill with built-in incentive to "spend" it in the manner you, the marketer, prefer.

Coupons benefit both the consumer and the marketer. Take advantage of them.

- **Standard information about your business or product.** Provide your hours of business, phone numbers, locations, product availability, etc. As your piece takes on reference value, people are more likely to keep it.

- **Customer testimonials.** One of the primary functions of your regular core mailings is to reinforce the purchase decision. We'll talk extensively about reinforcement in Chapter 21. For now, just be aware that client testimonials or usage stories are valuable.

- **Upcoming promotions or specials.** Pre-promote weeks, sometimes months, in advance. The Grateful Dead sells out concerts by pre-promoting to their core. You can do the same. By the time you begin hyping your upcoming promotion to the general public, your core may already have made plans to participate, buttressing the success of your promotion.

- **A recycling card or coupon.** When you recycle your customers, you're providing incentive for them to buy or patronize more often and at different times or days. Recycling is an important technique that warrants detailed discussion, and you'll read more about it in the next chapter.

For Major Core + Fringe Mailings

The following key ingredients should be included in every major core+fringe mailing:

- **An order blank or coupon.** The idea is to recruit new customers. You can get people to act by providing a vehicle for this, namely an order blank or a coupon.

- **Persuasive copy.** Beyond simply recruiting new patronage, your ultimate goal is to maintain that patronage long afterward. To that end, you should allocate space on your direct mail piece for some strongly written persuasion. Detailed information may or may not be appropriate (it depends on the nature of your product or service), but bottom-line information, written in a straightforward, concise manner, is always appropriate.

In some of your core+fringe mailings, though perhaps not all, you may want to include the following:

- **A contest.** The two primary objectives of a contest are to catch new customers or patrons who otherwise wouldn't respond and to increase or extend patronage of your existing or past customers. A well-conceived, well-executed contest accomplishes these objectives.

- **An entry blank or activator card.** When the recipient fills out an "activator card" or entry blank and mails it back or physically brings it in to your location, the respondent has committed to some form of subsequent patronage. In other words, he makes one decision—to fill out the entry card— then subsequently acts in accordance with that decision (such as returning to your store each day to see which card has been drawn, or tuning in to your commercial to see if his name is announced). With an activator card or entry blank, you reduce many recurring decisions, such as where to eat lunch each day, to one decision followed by corroborating action, such as returning to the same restaurant each day to see if one's entry blank has been chosen. This is how you create a buying habit.

- **A winning number.** A five- or six-digit number printed on a game piece is an alternative to an activator card or entry blank (participants compare their numbers with those drawn and designated as winners). However, a winning number doesn't prompt patronage commitment so strongly as an activator card or entry blank. In addition, you cannot collect names for your database with a winning number-type contest. But you can still run a good contest and recruit new patronage, which is the primary objective.

HOW TO INCREASE RESPONSE RATE

When people receive a direct mail piece, they run it through a series of mental questions in search of appropriate answers. As your piece answers each successive question, the piece moves along to the next question, making an impression each time and gaining in effectiveness along the way. When your piece fails to answer a question, it is rejected at that point and has no further effect.

Your objective is to answer all of the following four questions. You achieve that by designing your piece with the answers in prominent display. This mental questioning process happens subconsciously in the recipient's brain and with great speed. Therefore, your direct mail piece must provide the answers in a manner that can be received instantly by the brain. In other words, make them easy to see and grasp.

- **Question number one: "Who is sending this to me?"** Answer: Identify yourself as the sender, clearly and boldly. Some direct mailers believe the more nebulous or deceptive the outside of their piece appears, specifically regarding the true identity of the sender, the more impact and response it generates. While you may trick the recipient into opening the piece, as some marketers do with pieces that appear to be sent by some governmental organization, you ultimately hurt yourself by doing so. Hit-and-run marketers that rely on direct mail trickery may realize a short-term upward blip in response, but consequently realize much greater longer-term failure. Legitimate marketers need and strive for long-term customer satisfaction and repeat business, neither of which is achieved by tricking people.

- **Question number two: "What do I get from this?"** Answer: Give them the bottom line, what you are offering. If you elect to provide detailed information with your piece, fine. But don't require the reader to read through all the details to figure out what you're offering. Make sure the offer is stated in headline form, clearly and prominently.

- **Question number three: "What's it gonna cost me?"** Answer: Once again, state it clearly and prominently.

- **Question number four: "What do I do next?"** Answer: Tell the recipient exactly how to proceed. It's up to you to list the procedures, the exact steps you want the recipient to take.

"Fill out the entry card and mail it back," "Come to our store Saturday," "Call 555-345-6789 now." I'm suggesting the same writing style that appears in board games in which a player picks up a card that tells him exactly what to do next (as in "Advance to go and collect $200").

PART 4

LEVERAGING DEMAND

When you *leverage demand*, you're spreading demand to the masses—reaching and affecting hundreds, thousands, or millions of people. But leveraging is much more than simply spreading. When you leverage demand, you implement specific techniques that are *self-replicating* in nature. That is, once you have set your demand-leveraging systems in motion, demand then *spreads itself*, ultimating producing double, triple, or even 10 times the results you would otherwise realize! Leveraging demand is like pouring oil onto water. The oil subsequently spreads itself far and wide without any further effort on your part. This is the real secret to creating major demand. This is what shoots your demand jet to its highest altitude.

Each of the seven chapters in this part contains extremely powerful and effective demand-leveraging techniques. Some require such a low financial and manpower investment on your part they may appear weak or inconsequential. Do not be fooled by the deceptively simple nature of some of the demand-leveraging techniques we are about to discuss. Simplicity is part of their beauty, not to mention their budget-friendly nature, which I'm sure you can appreciate.

Chapter Thirteen

Get Your Customers to Buy More, More Often, through Recycling

W e'll start with one of the simplest demand leveraging techniques, *recycling*. Recycling techniques are extremely simple and easy to implement. You may be tempted to pass them up, thinking something so simple cannot produce a worthwhile result. I assure you, however, that the demand you create with simple recycling techniques will be well in excess of your investment in them.

THE RECYCLING CONCEPT

The idea behind recycling is to generate more purchases from your existing consumers or customers. When you coax a customer into buying again sooner, or buying another related product, or buying at a different time of day or time of year than she otherwise would without your coaxing, you're *recycling* your customer. Recycling is a proactive, rather than a reactive, process. You actively recycle your customers by implementing certain recycling techniques. You don't just sit back and hope they buy again someday. To recycle your customers, you must set things up so that each purchase is not an end in itself, but is *the first step toward the next purchase*. From the consumer's viewpoint, the purchase of your product or service provides a linkage to the next purchase, as when two people out on a date make plans to get together for a subsequent date.

Recycling Examples

As you know, the nightclub business is very trendy and cliquish. People can flock habitually to one place on one night of the week and another nightclub on another night of the week (preferring to be wherever things are "happening" on any given night). The nightclub in the present example has a great turnout every Wednesday night. In fact, the place is well known for being "the place to be" on Wednesday nights. But Friday nights are another story. For whatever reason, Friday night is sparse. Here's how the nightclub became packed on Friday nights in less than three weeks after instituting their recycling program. On one Wednesday night, they handed each person who came through the door a special "VIP Card." The cardboard card, about the size of a credit card, offered free admission for two on any Friday night before 10 P.M. (the club normally charges a $2 cover). In addition, the card could be redeemed for one free drink on Friday night. The result? Some people from the Wednesday night crowd came back on Friday night. It took only two Wednesday nights to produce an overflow crowd on Friday nights.

But the nightclub didn't drop their recycling program once they had achieved their goal. They have VIP Cards printed in different card colors for different nights of the week, and they pass out a batch periodically, though not regularly (on some Fridays, for example, they pass out cards that are good for Tuesday nights; on some Tuesdays they pass out cards good for Thursday nights, etc.).

Let's analyze the finer points of this recycling program. By making *each card* good for free admission for *two*, they encouraged each cardholder to bring a friend (this is an example of the encouraged endorsement technique we'll cover in the next chapter). Free admission before 10 P.M. encouraged people to arrive relatively early. This precondition accomplished two very important objectives. First, it headed people off who would otherwise have gone to another nightclub initially. Second, it got the place packed early, giving the later arrivals the impression that the place was crowded and "happening." The free drink redemption value also accomplished two important objectives. First, it gave the cardholder a reward for coming and a reason to stay while consuming a free drink (preventing the early arrivals from simply cruising through and leaving as fast as they came). Second, it jump-started the bar as the cardholder got a free drink and bought one for a friend. Notice also that the card must be turned in to get the free drink. To get another card, one would have to come back on another night (although on this particular night one might have been handed a similar card that is good on another night).

The dry cleaner I go to recycles with a "Special Customer Card." Each time I have shirts laundered, the clerk punches a hole in another number on the card, representing the number of shirts I had cleaned. When the number 50 is reached, I may then redeem the card to have three shirts laundered at no charge.

Notice that recycling not only can inspire customers to increase their purchases of your product or service, but it can also reduce the chances of them patronizing a competitor. When you recycle, you're giving your customer an *equity interest* in the next purchase. Suddenly your product or service is more valuable than a competitor's, since the buyer now possesses some equity in yours. Who wants to throw away equity? The "use it or lose it" reasoning takes hold, and the buyer favors you and purchases again.

Broadcasters use recycling techniques all the time. Radio stations constantly are "cross-promoting" different dayparts (times of the day). This means the morning announcers are asking you to tune in during the afternoon. The afternoon announcers tease you with something happening on the air later that night. The nighttime announcers ask you to set your clock radio to wake up to the station in the morning.

Did you ever hear a radio station run some kind of call-in contest in which they give you the answer to a particular question in the afternoon and ask you to listen the following morning for the question (and your chance to call in and win)? When you receive the answer in the afternoon, you have equity in the morning show, so you tune in mornings to take advantage of it. You've just been recycled.

Television stations, including the networks, are constantly recycling. They're always promoting shows to be broadcast the following evening or following week. (The rating services break the ratings into weekly races, so it's important for the networks to recycle viewers from one week to the next as well as from one day to the next.) Remember when almost every TV show ended with scenes from next week's episode? That type of recycling is used to a much lesser degree today. It makes less sense to recycle viewers to the same show (which would probably happen anyway without the tease) because it's more effective to recycle viewers to other shows in other time periods or other days or weeks. Instead of scenes from an upcoming episode of the show you just watched, you'll see scenes and promos for different shows.

Here's an example of recycling on a major, nationwide basis. For many years, McDonald's ran their Monopoly contest every spring. With each contest piece you acquired, not only could you be an instant winner of a small prize such as a cheeseburger, fries, or Coke, but also you could become a big winner of a major cash prize by *accumulating* game pieces that make up a complete set, all four railroads, for example. Each piece gives you equity in the set it belongs to. Of course, you must keep returning to McDonald's to accumulate additional pieces to complete your set. McDonald's runs other contests from time to time that are different in theme and concept, but they all have one element in common: recycling.

THE IMPORTANCE OF RECYCLING

If you let a consumer purchase your product or service, or let a customer leave your store, without receiving a recycling card, you're forfeiting future business. Conversely, every time you get a recycling card into the hands of a customer or consumer, you're increasing the odds of that person buying again. Get a lot of recycling cards out and your sales are affected dramatically.

Many marketers are disheartened by the fact that so many consumers do not care what brand of product or service they purchase. One brand is just as good as the next to a lot of people. What can make a consumer with no strong brand preference suddenly adopt a strong brand preference? Equity in the next purchase. And what provides that equity? A recycling card. It makes so much sense and costs so little to implement, you should never be without a good recycling program in effect at all times.

HOW TO IMPLEMENT RECYCLING

As you can see, recycling is easy to implement. If you follow these four steps, you'll have recycling working for you in no time:

- **Step 1. Determine what specific behavior you wish to occur.** Would you like your customers to return again within the week, month, or year? Would you like them to purchase a related product or service? You must be specific. "I would like them to buy my brand again the next time they need toothpaste," is too general. "I would like them to buy another tube within 60 days (of the first purchase)" is better.

- **Step 2. Provide equity.** The first thing that may come to mind is to offer a monetary discount (i.e., "$1 off your next purchase"). That's okay, but not quite so strong as offering a bonus product or service.

  Your product or service itself is a great source of equity. The nightclub I talked about earlier offered a free Friday admission and a free Friday drink to each Wednesday night patron. The Friday admission and drink are the equity. They are much stronger than offering a discount on admission and drink. The main difference is in how it's worded, whether you place your emphasis on the item received (stronger) or the amount of money saved (weaker).

- **Step 3. Make it tangible.** It's not enough to ask people to buy again verbally or in print. You must practically put your recycling into their hands. This means you must make it tangible. Create a recycling card or note. Give it a name as the nightclub ("VIP Card") and dry cleaner ("Special Customer Card") did. Make sure the equity you're offering is stated clearly on the card.

    Another way to make your recycling tangible is to add equity to something that is already tangible, as McDonald's does with their game pieces. The entire game is built around recycling. Each tangible game piece is part of a potentially winning set, thus it contains equity.

- **Step 4. Provide your recycling card at the time of purchase.** Remember, to recycle people you must make each purchase the first step toward the next purchase. Making recycling-type offers in your ads or commercials is not recycling. Nor is indiscriminately passing out your recycling cards on the street corner. To procure a recycling card, a person must make a purchase.

Chapter Fourteen

Turn Customers
into Persuaders

T he idea is to inspire your customers to recruit new customers for you—like a church that encourages its congregation to go out and "spread the word" and bring in new church members. Like the nightclub we discussed in the last chapter that made each recycling card good for free admission for two, so the recipient would bring a friend. The technique is called *encouraged endorsement* (the marketer encourages the customer to endorse). When you encourage endorsement of your product or service, you are empowering each of your customers to assist you in the demand creation process. It's as though you "deputize" your customers and make them pseudo-members of your sales staff.

You can encourage two different types of endorsement, *aggressive* and *passive*. They're quite different, so we'll discuss them separately, beginning with encouraged aggressive endorsement.

ENCOURAGED AGGRESSIVE ENDORSEMENT

Aggressive endorsement occurs when one person persuades another to patronize your establishment, or to buy your product or service. In this sense, aggressive endorsement can also be called recommendation. Here are some examples.

A lawnmower marketer offered a $25 limited-time rebate on a particular model. The buyer was required to fill out and return a special rebate card inserted in the instruction manual (another way of collecting names for the database). The rebate card was actually two cards, perforated down the middle. The buyer returned one, and the other card read, "Know a friend, neighbor, or relative who could use a new Acme lawnmower? Do him or her a favor. Give him this card, good for $25 off a brand new Acme Model 123." This card asks the buyer deliberately to recommend the Acme brand of lawnmower by giving another person the discount card.

Columbia House record club sends its members a pamphlet with this offer: Sign up a friend and you get three compact discs or four cassettes free. Part of the pamphlet is a membership application; fill in your friend's name, tear the card off at the perforation, and mail it in. Actually, there are two membership applications provided, in case you want to get six CDs or eight cassettes free by signing up two friends.

Geico Insurance sends its policy holders a pamphlet with this heading: "Why should YOU help your friends to save more with GEICO?" It then provides reasons for doing so. It even has a three-panel cartoon showing one person giving the pamphlet, which contains an application form, to a neighbor.

Two earlier examples also fall into the aggressive endorsement category: the church that encourages its members to recruit others, and the nightclub that passes out recycling cards encouraging each recipient to bring a friend or date when returning on Friday. (Recycling and encouraged endorsement work well together. Often you can implement both techniques with one card.)

ENCOURAGED PASSIVE ENDORSEMENT

Passive endorsement occurs when a person displays use of a particular product or service. The key word is display. The display of usage is seen by others, who are in turn influenced to do the same. If you encourage it properly, passive endorsement happens automatically, without the initial buyer making any deliberate recommendation.

One of the best examples of passive endorsement can be seen on the back of every pickup truck. Just about every pickup manufacturer puts the company or brand name on the tailgate. And not just painted on, but embossed in the metal. And not in small letters. When you buy a pickup truck, you're displaying the make you've chosen for the world to see, every minute you're on the road and every minute it's parked in your driveway. Kind of makes you want to send good ol' Ford, Chevrolet, or Toyota a bill for your endorsement services, doesn't it?

Many clothing marketers encourage passive endorsement by making sure their logos are prominently visible on their products. Lacoste's alligator, Polo's polo player, and Levi's pocket tag are a few examples.

Clothing is a great vehicle for encouraging passive endorsement even if you're not primarily a clothing marketer. Every time people wear a piece of Coca-Cola clothing, they're endorsing the drink. Harley-Davidson motorcycles is into logo-laden clothing now, too. Maybe a lot more people than motorcycle riders will wear the clothes and thereby passively endorse the motorcycle, whether they own one or not.

Notice that passive endorsement is much more than simple logo exposure. When the consumer *displays his usage*, he is implying support; he is putting his personal "stamp of approval" on the product. It's not the name "Ford" on your tailgate that does the trick; it's you, driving the Ford in public, that makes the difference. You needn't be any kind of celebrity, either. Your friends and co-workers know you personally, which says enough to them. Strangers see the way you come across, and that tells them what type of people to associate with that product. Endorsement carries much greater influence power than simple logo exposure.

WHY PEOPLE ENDORSE

Why would a person want to endorse a product or service? Asked another way, what incentive is needed to get a person to aggressively or passively endorse your product or service?

A person will engage in endorsement activity for any of the following reasons:

- **To gain higher status.** The endorser displays her allegiance to a particular product or service as a means of bonding with the type of people the product or service represents. This is another way of saying she wants status to transfer from the product to herself.

  Also, an endorser may raise his status by appearing knowledgeable and experienced. An act of aggressive endorsement puts the endorser in a position of strength in the eyes of the person he's talking to.

- **To share experiences.** It's instinctive for humans to want to share experiences. We want others to experience that which we find pleasurable.

- **To gain reinforcement.** People don't always feel confident with every purchase decision they make. One way a person gains positive reinforcement regarding a recent purchase is to recommend the same product or service to another. If the other person sees value in it and buys, it makes the first person feel better about his purchase. (We'll discuss reinforcement itself in Chapter 21.)

Now that you know why people endorse, you can encourage endorsement with the proper incentives and make it happen.

HOW TO ENCOURAGE AGGRESSIVE ENDORSEMENT

- **Step 1: Create an endorsement card or pamphlet.** An endorsement card is similar to a recycling card. In fact, a single card can be both a recycling card and an endorsement card if the card contains both recycling and endorsing elements. Like recycling, aggressive endorsement occurs much more often when you use a tangible card or pamphlet.

- **Step 2: Use wording that inspires the recipient to aggressively endorse.** People need an incentive to recommend your product or service to another. The best incentives you can offer satisfy the buyer's need to gain status, share experiences, or have her purchase decision reinforced.

Geico's pamphlet encourages aggressive endorsement by pointing out the great favor you'll be performing when you help your friend save money on his automobile insurance. That's the gaining status motive.

Here are two examples that play on the sharing of experiences.

"SPECIAL PATRON TICKET. Two free drinks with any dinner. Treat yourself and a guest to the Acme dining experience. Valid any Monday after 7 P.M. during the month of June."

"Double your fun! Take a friend along the next time you visit your favorite Acme Toy dealer. When you buy two or more of the *same* accessory, we'll give *each* of you $2 off!"

Here's one that uses reinforcement as the main incentive:

"One of the greatest benefits to owning Acme carpeting is seeing how others enjoy its superb feel and decorative beauty when they visit. When anyone asks, or pays you a compliment, as they undoubtedly will, be sure to tell them it's Acme Carpeting they're enjoying. Pass along the attached card as well. It will entitle the recipient to the same ONE FREE ROOM OF PADDING you received. Smart homeowners like you choose Acme when they want the very best."

- **Step 3: Include an encouraged endorsement card with every item purchased.** Or send them out with your next core-directed database mailing.

HOW TO ENCOURAGE PASSIVE ENDORSEMENT

- **The one and only step: Attach your logo to your product in a highly visible position.** It does you little good to have people buying and using your product if other people cannot instantly determine it's your product they're using. It's up to you to make sure your logo is visible. Passive endorsement is not going to happen if you leave it up to the customer to seek out your logo and display it somehow. (Throughout this book I've offered various tips to pull a commodity item out of the quagmire, and this is another one. Attach a logo to a commodity item, and the item is no longer such a commodity. That's exactly how blue jeans became designer jeans. And how Chiquita differentiated its bananas from other brands.)

How do you attach a logo to a service? It's a bit more difficult than with a product, but there are ways. Construction companies will often put a large sign in front of the site they're building to let the public know the developer has engaged their firm to build. Chemlawn parks its flashy truck in front of your house for all your neighbors to see.

Some services are not conducive to encouraged endorsement because people do not want it known they're using certain services. Not many people would be willing to walk around wearing a sticker on their jackets displaying the name of "Dr. Joe Doe—Plastic Surgery," for example.

Although I maintain fairly high visibility as a writer and speaker, I'm forced to conduct actual consulting services in a very low profile, sometimes clandestine, fashion. Few people want it known they're bringing in a management consultant (other than for a speaking engagement), and virtually no one will display any such usage. If your service is not conducive to usage display, you may find it difficult to encourage endorsement. But if you do invent a way, let me know.

Chapter Fifteen

Harness the Power of Human Influence

You're going to enjoy this chapter. It deals with the essence of human influence, how each of us is influenced by others to behave as we do. You'll learn how individual people influence one another and how influence as a whole travels through the population over time. You'll learn how your marketing and human influence work together to create demand. In fact, you'll learn exactly how to tap into the tremendous power of human influence to create an incredible level of demand for your product or service!

Think about this: Without human influence, almost no behavioral changes would ever occur. One person would arbitrarily adopt a new behavior, wearing a different style of shoe for example, and no one else would be influenced to do the same. The new shoe style would never catch on or spread. We'd all be dressing today the same as our forefathers did a couple hundred years ago (or for that matter, the way the Romans did thousands of years ago).

When you stop to think about it, you realize that human influence is really a pervasive force in society, for all humans are constantly both influencing others and being influenced by others. Human influence, therefore, affects virtually every aspect of human behavior, including the purchase and use of all products and services.

We can conclude, therefore, that the level of demand for your specific product or service is affected greatly by human influence. It is affected greatly by each person that influences another (or many others) either to buy your product or not. Thus the level of demand for your product is being affected by human influence right now, every minute of every day, in one way or another, whether you have anything to do with that influence or not. Given that fact, it obviously behooves you to harness human influence and get it working for you, rather than simply ignore it and accept whatever consequence occurs.

THE STYLE, ART, AND FASHION (SAF) FACTOR

Human influence is most acute and visible in the area of *style, art,* and *fashion,* or *SAF.* The *SAF Factor* plays a very important role in the entire human influence process, the many reasons for which I will be noting throughout this discussion. Here's the first reason now:

The SAF Factor provides a means by which we can differentiate among different types of people. You see, while all humans are alike in that we are constantly both influencing others and being influenced by others, we differ from one another in our *receptivity of newness* in the SAF area. In other words, some people are very receptive to new style, art, and fashion, and adopt quickly behavior that displays this receptivity. Other people are averse to new style, art, and fashion and adopt things that display these slowly.

You must understand exactly what *new* or *newness* means in the SAF area. If you buy a brand new suit, yet the suit is very similar in design and overall appearance to most other suits that have been worn by people for years, you are not displaying newness. But if the suit is the latest style and looks significantly different from most other suits, it's new. If you purchase a painting by an unknown artist whose work appears very similar to that of other established artists, you are displaying a very low level of newness. If you purchase a painting from an artist who has been around for a while, yet whose work appears vastly different from anything else out there, you are displaying a high level of newness. SAF newness is not necessarily that which never existed before. If the latest style of tie is significantly thinner than what the majority of men are wearing, the thinner tie is new, even though thin ties have existed before.

Before we move on, let me stop you from jumping to the possible conclusion that your particular product or service has nothing to do with style, art, or fashion, and, therefore, this material is not applicable. I can assure you that whatever the nature of your product or service, the SAF Factor plays a major role in its marketing success. This will become evident below.

THE FOUR INFLUENCE TYPES

All humans fall into one of four Influence Types, based on their receptivity to newness in the areas of style, art, and fashion. As we discuss each type, please keep in mind that we are not judging people or attaching any relative values to the classifications we create. The differences we use to categorize people have nothing to do with intelligence level or personality. We attach no right or wrong, good or bad, values to these categories. I cannot emphasize this point enough. The last thing the world needs is another measure that encourages prejudice based on differences among people, and I'm not about to supply one. However, I am introducing a new measure by which marketers may distinguish among consumer preferences simply as a means of better serving the consumer. Marketers that keep any personal biases out of this system will benefit greatly by it.

Type One

Type One people are extremely aware of, and receptive to, new style, art, and fashion. As a matter of fact, they actively seek it. By nature, Type Ones not only welcome SAF newness, but also often create it. Consequently, they are very quick to adopt new behavior. Type Ones view themselves as people on the cutting-edge, the trend setters. They thrive on being different and often display their uniqueness in a variety of ways. Type Ones constitute about 10 percent of the earth's population.

Type Two

Like Type Ones, Type Twos are also receptive to newness in style, art, and fashion and welcome it. Unlike Type Ones, however, who seek new SAF as naturally as breathing, Type Twos find their receptivity somewhat strained. They make the effort to seek new SAF because the effort is enjoyable, but it is an effort nonetheless. Although Type Twos rely on others to start trends, Type Twos will adopt, and thereby perpetuate, a trend fairly early. Type Twos constitute about 20 percent of the earth's population.

Type Three

Unlike Types One and Two who actively seek SAF newness, Type Threes exert minimal effort. Type Threes do not believe it is up to them to reach out to new SAF; rather, they wait for new SAF to reach them. As a consequence, Type Threes are exposed to less new SAF than Types One and Two—their awareness is much lower—and that's fine with them. As you might expect, Type Threes are slower to adopt new SAF behavior than Types One and Two. Type Threes constitute about 40 percent of the earth's population.

Type Four

Type Fours are very averse to SAF newness. They are often unaware of or oblivious to many forms of SAF newness because they limit their exposure to it. They place little or no value on new SAF, and exert no effort to get it. To many other people, Type Fours seem "behind the times." They adopt trends long after trends have been around and are extremely slow to drop old SAF behavior. Type Fours constitute about 30 percent of the earth's population.

IDENTIFYING INFLUENCE TYPE

The very first thing you must do is develop the ability to equate people with Influence Type. You must have a feel for what Influence Type various people fall into. This will enable you to determine the Influence Type(s) of your own consumers or customers, as well as the Type(s) you might want to attract.

The primary way to ascertain Influence Type is through *constant observation*. Remember, the SAF Factor is the underlying determinant. How readily people accept newness of style, art, and fashion indicates what Influence Type they are. Display of SAF newness is what you're looking for. Here are the particulars.

Appearance is the most obvious Influence Type indicator. Clothing, hairstyle, and accessories (including style of glasses, if they are worn) can tell you a lot. Note people's entertainment preferences in the SAF area—the music or recording artists they like, the movies they prefer, the magazines they read. The type of car they drive, the way their home is decorated, and the restaurants they frequent are also tip-offs.

Sex and age are irrelevant, though with the latter it might appear otherwise. As people age, the form in which they express their SAF preferences changes. A 20-year-old Type One might wear vastly different clothing from a 40-year-old Type One, who might wear vastly different clothing from a 60-year-old Type One. While a 20-year-old Type One might have just bought a CD of a new, esoteric rock band no one else has ever heard of, a 50-year-old Type One might have just attended the latest Kronos Quartet concert.

People tend to drift in the One-to-Four direction as they age. Thus a Type Two may become a Type Three, or a Type Three may become a Type Four as they get older. As people age, they become less willing to put forth the same level of effort to accept SAF newness as they once did. Of course, some people can do the opposite and move in the Four-to-One direction. They can reach a certain age and suddenly experience a personal renaissance, displaying a heightened effort to accept SAF newness. But this is rare. Despite this drift, the relative proportions of each Influence Type (Ones, 10 percent; Twos, 20 percent; Threes, 40 percent;

Fours, 30 percent) hold true in the aggregate. In fact, within any age range, 30 to 40 for example, the percentages of Influence Type hold true.

Start with yourself, since you know yourself best. What Influence Type are you? Consider other people you know. What Influence Type is your husband, wife, boyfriend, girlfriend, best friend, or boss? You will need to identify the Influence Type not only of certain individuals, such as the people who appear in your ads and commercials, but also of large segments of the population, such as your present consumers or customers (groups can fall into specific Influence Types just as individuals do). Developing the ability to ascertain Influence Type is not difficult once you get a feel for it. A little practice is all it takes. Caution: Any one or two indicators may not be enough. Rarely can you simply look at someone and conclude, "He's a One," or "She's a Three." It takes constant observation of a number of indicators.

Incidentally, the worst way to ascertain Influence Type is to explain all this to someone and ask him what Type he is, or even to mention what type you think he is. Despite cautions against doing so, people tend instinctively to attach values to the various Types, and they become very defensive about where they fall—as though you're asking them to tell you their inmost secret.

THE INFLUENCE GRAPH

Let's examine a visual layout of the four Influence Types. In Figure 2 you'll see each Influence Type placed side by side on what's called The Influence Graph. The Influence Graph brings into play two very important elements that affect human influence, direction and time. Specifically, it shows how influence moves or flows from one Type to the next over time. It is a big-picture view of influence moving through the population.

How the Influence Graph Works

A behavior, the purchase of a product or service, for example, can begin with any Influence Type. The actual spot on the graph where a particular product or service gains initial acceptance

FIGURE 2
The Influence Graph

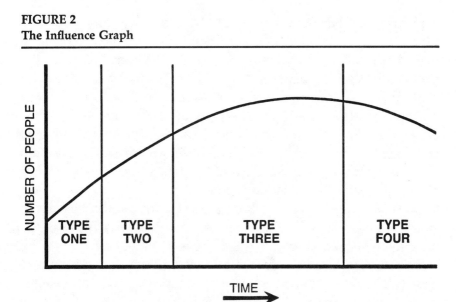

Influence travels from left to right over time.

depends on the nature of the item and the nature of its marketing. But regardless of where adoptive behavior starts, it moves from that point to the right. It does not move to the left of its initial starting point.

Let's follow one actual behavior as it moves through The Influence Graph. We'll use a real-life example from the music industry. The behavior is the purchase of musical product (lps, cassettes, CDs) of the rock group U2.

In 1980 U2 enjoyed tremendous popularity with Type Ones in the United States. Of course, even with Type One acceptance they sold a relatively small amount of product, since Type Ones represent only 10 percent of the total population. The majority of the population hadn't even heard of U2 back then.

As time went on and Type Ones displayed adoption of U2, Type Twos became influenced. Twos began buying U2 product, resulting in significantly greater sales by 1983 (Twos are 20 percent of the population). Up to this point, U2 received virtually no exposure on CHR (Contemporary Hit Radio) stations, and very little exposure on AOR (Album Oriented Rock) stations. However, MTV, which was targeted to Types One and Two at the time, embraced the band and gave them plenty of exposure. By 1984, Type Two influence began to reach some Type Threes (those on the left side of the Type Three range). Once a recording artist crosses the line between the Type Two and Type Three ranges, the artist becomes "legitimate" as far as many mass-appeal radio stations are concerned. In 1984, U2 began to receive some CHR airplay and substantial AOR airplay.

By 1987, when U2's new album *The Joshua Tree* was released, the stage had been set for Type Three acceptance. Mass-appeal radio stations, which are targeted to Type Threes, had no problem playing singles from the album. As influence permeated throughout the Type Three range, sales of U2 product really took off (Threes represent a whopping 40 percent of the total population). By the summer of 1987, U2 had two number-one songs under their belt. As time went on, Type Fours began buying U2 product. By the fall of 1988, *The Joshua Tree* had sold over 5 million copies (and is still selling).

While U2's popularity was spreading throughout the Three and Four ranges, however, a very interesting consequence developed. The Ones began abandoning the band. As the Ones are fond of saying, "If it sells, it smells." Or "They (the artist) sold out." Why do Ones feel this way? As we discussed in Chapter 5, people will associate and disassociate with things based on the level of status an item provides. Type Ones have a self image of being trend-setters, of being the supreme arbiters of acceptable SAF. They feel compelled to radiate uniqueness, which represents status to them. They take pride in their individuality and will associate with things that reinforce it... mainly things that the rest of the population does not embrace. When something becomes accepted by a growing number of others, Ones feel compelled to disassociate.

Of course, the shunning behavior Ones display influences Twos to do the same. Eventually the shunning of a product or service can work its way through the population the same as the adoption of a product or service. U2's next album after *The Joshua Tree*, called *Rattle and Hum*, didn't sell nearly as well.

How the Influence Graph Affects Sales

Okay, you launched a new product, and Type Ones have begun buying it. (Again, let me point out initial acceptance can begin with any Influence Type. But to illustrate how sales are affected throughout each range, we'll assume your new product appeals to Type Ones initially).

Type Ones represent only 10 percent of the population. Even if every Type One in your trading area bought your new product, which isn't very likely, you'd still rack up relatively few sales. Often a marketer launches a new product and soon becomes disappointed with marketplace acceptance because the majority of the population doesn't immediately embrace it. That's a big mistake. If your new product or service has a strong Type One appeal, and Type Ones accept it, you have a very successful launch on your hands. The majority of the population isn't supposed to buy your product yet. That comes later.

As influence moves into the Type Two range over time, your sales begin to increase. Then influence hits the Type Three range. As it permeates throughout the Three range, Ones begin shunning. You're trading One acceptance for Three acceptance. Since there are four times as many Threes as Ones, your sales are really taking off, even though you're losing One acceptance.

Eventually Fours start adopting and Twos start shunning. Now you're trading Two acceptance for Four acceptance, which results in still higher sales, since Fours outnumber Twos. At this point many marketers get a false sense of success. They're oblivious to the problem of Ones and Twos shunning because overall sales figures are still rising. (This is why it's so important to identify the Type of people buying your product or service.) Then the shunning influence moves into the left side of the Three range and sales begin to drop. As more and more Threes shun, and no other Influence Type begins adopting to replace the shunners (Ones will not adopt so long as Fours still do), your sales really nosedive. Many a marketer has helplessly watched sales drop without ever understanding why. Now you know.

By the way, there are a few instances in which influence does live throughout all Influence Types at the same time. Pepsi, Madonna, the movie *Batman*, Levi's, and McDonald's are a few examples. In these cases, Type Ones do not shun the product even though Types Three and Four adopt it. The reason for this, including specific steps you can take to extend the life of your product or service, will be addressed in the next chapter.

RESISTANCE BARRIERS

In our examples so far, we watched influence flow from one Type to the next without any problem. In reality, there is resistance in the system that inhibits the flow of influence at times.

Here's how a *resistance barrier* can impede the growth of a product's marketplace acceptance. The television series "Twin Peaks" made its debut in early 1990 on the ABC network and quickly became the buzz of the nation. You couldn't live through 1990 without being exposed to media publicity and street talk about the show. With that kind of adoptive behavior on display, you'd expect influence to flow through the entire Influence Graph in no time, making the show one of the most watched shows in the country, wouldn't you? Yet "Twin Peaks" consistently languished in the bottom third of all network shows in the ratings. Why? The show hit a resistance barrier between the Type Two and Three ranges, and adoptive influence never moved into the Type Three range.

Here's why: "Twin Peaks" required the viewer to exert an effort to understand and appreciate it. It was avant-garde, artsy, and subtle. It exuded the SAF newness that Types One and Two seek and appreciate. They embraced the show without hesitation. Types Three and Four, on the other hand, do not value SAF newness and make no effort to obtain it. Threes and Fours never made the effort to understand or appreciate "Twin Peaks." When you have a television show that garners only Type One and Two appeal, it will never generate high ratings (Ones and Twos combined represent only 30 percent of the population).

Resistance barriers can pop up at various places on The Influence Graph. Some products never develop any appeal past the Type One range. Some, like "Twin Peaks," fail to move into the Type Three range. Others fade in the Type Three range and never gain any Type Four acceptance. Resistance barriers also can appear in the middle of a Type range. The appeal of *GQ* magazine, for example, fades out in the middle of the Type Three range.

Resistance barriers exist because a particular level of SAF newness may be just too much for Types farther down the line to accept, no matter how much time goes by. *GQ* will not appeal to people in the half-of-Three through Four range, now or ever.

HOW THE SAF FACTOR RELATES TO YOUR PRODUCT OR SERVICE AND ITS MARKETING

Let's say your particular product or service is, by nature, *SAF-intensive*. That is, it inherently contains elements of style, art, and fashion. Examples include, but are not limited to, such things as clothing, recorded music, home furnishings, beauty aids, live entertainment of all varieties, books, movies, television programs, decorative items, radio stations, etc. With such products or services, it is obvious how marketplace acceptance is affected by consumer SAF tastes.

But what if your product or service is *SAF-light*? What if it inherently has little to do with style, art, and fashion? Examples include, but are not limited to, such things as power and hand tools, life insurance, grocery items, fast food, legal services, garden hoses, etc. If human influence revolves around SAF, and your product is SAF-light, then how is your product affected by human influence?

The answer is quite intriguing. Even if your product is SAF-light, the *marketing of* your product or service, especially in the advertising area, is SAF-intensive. Marketing is, by nature, SAF-intensive. In fact, advertising itself is a form of SAF expression. You may be the manufacturer or retailer of an SAF-light item such as a pipe wrench, but when you market your pipe wrench, you're suddenly dealing with SAF in a big way, whether you intend to be or not. (Some products seem to be SAF-intensive, but when you stop to analyze, you notice they are actually SAF-light. Beer and cigarettes are cases in point. Their marketing is so SAF-intensive it causes the SAF qualities to rub off onto the product itself.)

Together, your product and its marketing portray a particular level of SAF newness, whether that level is high or low. In the case of SAF-light products and services, the marketing component carries the heavier load of SAF. But regardless of which component—your product or your marketing—delivers what percentage of the SAF, make no mistake about it: Your product and its marketing are telegraphing a certain level of SAF newness, high or low. And that level of SAF newness is determining what Type of people you're appealing to, and how much overall demand you're creating.

Get out your marker and circle that last paragraph. It's vitally important.

THE SAF FACTOR HAS A PROFOUND EFFECT ON PEOPLE

To understand why the SAF Factor affects demand for your product or service so strongly, look at what happens at the consumer's end.

Every single person is innately aware of the SAF nuances of every product or service and its marketing that he is exposed to. This innate awareness is deeply subconscious most of the time. But its effects are extremely powerful. Here's why. When the level of SAF newness that your product and its marketing exudes matches that which a particular consumer wants, a little "comfort button" in the subconscious part of her brain is activated. Without knowing why (or bothering even to think about it), she simply *feels comfortable* with your product or service. She feels your item is for her. It's as if she is magically drawn to it. On the other hand, if the level of SAF newness you are exuding does not match a particular person's desires, a "discomfort button" is activated. Without knowing why, the person experiences *uncomfortable feelings* about your product or service. He feels your item is just not for him. He is mysteriously repelled by it. The SAF Factor is an enigmatic, powerful force that either draws people toward your product or repels people from it.

MATCHING SAF NEWNESS WITH INFLUENCE TYPE

When the particular level of SAF newness exuded by your product/service and its marketing matches a particular Influence Type, people of that Type and those near them on The Influence Graph will be attracted. When your level of SAF newness differs from a particular Influence Type, people of that Type, and those close to them on The Influence Graph, will be repelled. Here are some examples.

Have you ever felt uncomfortable in a particular restaurant and not known why? The food and service may be fine, but for some reason you just don't like dining there. Could it be the restaurant exudes a level of SAF newness different from your Influence Type? The next time you enter a restaurant, observe its level of SAF newness. Start by noticing its location. Neighborhoods can be classified by Influence Type based on the Type of people that tend to live there. Is this restaurant located in a Type One section of town? (Type One and Type Two neighborhoods are almost never located in suburbia, by the way.) Or is it in a Type Three section? Pay attention to the decor, the way the employees are dressed, the way the menu is designed, the way the other customers appear. Chances are you'll see a definite match between the degree of SAF newness of the place and the Influence Type(s) who are eating there.

Incidentally, restaurants and other retail establishments must be very careful to match their location and degree of SAF newness. I've seen a fine Type Two-appeal restaurant go out of business because it was located in a Type Four section of town and a fine Type Four-appeal restaurant fail because it was in a Type One and Two section of town.

The SAF Factor affects all retail establishments, not just restaurants. Walk into any department store, hardware store, supermarket, hair salon, whatever, and either your subconscious comfort button or discomfort button will be activated.

Here's an interesting occurrence. A friend of mine was having a hard time selling her house. People were looking, but no one was biting. She was perplexed greatly, for the house was in fine shape and her asking price was very reasonable. I took one look at the inside of the house and knew immediately what the problem was. The house exuded a low degree of SAF newness, yet it was located in a Type One section of town.

"Paint the foyer and the living room walls purple," I suggested (they were a dull beige).

"Purple?" she repeated somewhat incredulously.

"Actually, the name of the paint color is Periwinkle," I explained. "It's a vibrant, lavenderish purple."

Since I could see she wasn't crazy about the idea, I delivered the Consultant's Oldest Line (which I'm convinced Nike must have picked up from one of my colleagues somewhere). "Just do it," I said on the way out. She wasn't any crazier about painting the walls purple after hearing the Consultant's Oldest Line, but when your explanation is only three words long, people do seem to pause and ponder.

A week later she informed me she was in the process of painting the walls Periwinkle. "Are you sure this is going to work?" she queried.

One day not long after, she was on the phone sounding so excited I figured she either had sold the house or was calling to warn me to get out of town before she came over to kill me.

"You're not going to believe what happened," she exclaimed. "The first couple to see the house bought, and they said they were interested within the first 30 seconds . . . before they'd gotten even halfway into the living room!"

Of course, that wouldn't have happened if the couple had been either Type Three or Four. But since the house was in a Type

One section of town, the odds were Ones and Twos would be looking to live there. By painting the first two rooms Periwinkle, my friend simply altered the SAF newness of the house to match Type One and Two preferences better.

Matching Your SAF Newness with Desired Influence Type

There are a number of questions you must answer about your own situation. Here are a few of the more important ones.

Are your present consumers or customers of the Type you expect or desire? Marketers are often surprised to find out the Type of people who are attracted to their product or service is very different from what they expected. Which means the level of SAF newness they're exuding is either too high or too low to appeal to the Type the marketer expects or desires.

Are you doing all you can to increase your desired Type's comfort level? Is your product or service itself designed to exude just the right level of SAF newness? Check its color(s), shape, and form. How about your packaging? Color(s), shape, form, wording, and style of type all telegraph a certain level of SAF newness.

If you have a physical location, do your customers seem comfortable or uncomfortable in your place? Do they like to spend time browsing, or do they breeze in and out as quickly as they can? Do they appear happy, relaxed, and interested, or expressionless, stiff, and bored? Through constant observation, you can tell whether you're activating their comfort buttons or not. You'll be amazed at how some slight alterations in your SAF newness can increase their comfort level tremendously. Check your lighting, shelf design, and floor layout. The type of background music you have is vitally important. How are your employees dressed? Remember, every detail has an effect.

Matching in Your Personal Life

I know this is a marketing book, but I'm going to take a minute to show you how matching in the SAF and Influence Type areas affects your personal life. Consider this a bonus section.

I asked you earlier to identify your own Influence Type, along with that of your spouse or boyfriend/girlfriend. Do they match, or are you and your significant other mismatched? If you're both the same Influence Type, chances are you'll feel a strong and deep level of comfort with one another. Your entertainment choices, house decorating tastes, and restaurant preferences will be virtually alike. Each of you will prefer to live in the same type of house, in the same type of neighborhood. You'll have very similar philosophies of how kids should be reared, and you'll agree on the style of clothes you purchase for the kids. Each of you may find that the other seems to have some mysterious quality or ability to bring out the best in you.

If the two of you are of the same Type, yet at opposite ends of the range (i.e., a left-sided Three and a right-sided Three), or are of different Types that are adjacent (i.e., a right-sided One and a left-sided Two), an interesting relationship will surely develop. One of you, the Type farther to the left on The Influence Graph, constantly will be adopting newer SAF behavior, and the other person constantly will be influenced to do likewise—no problem, though the adoption of new behavior may spark a little discussion and debate at times.

But suppose the two of you are a full Type-range apart (i.e., a right-sided Two and a right-sided Three; a left-sided Three and a left-sided Four)? The distance may present problems. Each of you may develop uncomfortable feelings about the other or may become frustrated with the other's adoptive behavior at times. Potential long-term problems could result.

I once watched a Type Three male grow increasingly dissatisfied with his relationship. He didn't know exactly why this dissatisfaction existed, because his girlfriend was, by his own admission, kind, considerate, caring, and committed. But he did notice they spent a lot of time arguing about the appropriateness of each other's dress, for one thing. He knew he was becoming less and less comfortable with her as time went on. One day he met a new girl, and in a flash he backstroked out of the first relationship and dove into a new one. Soon he started dressing differently and going out more. The two went everywhere together, they seemed to fire each other up with energy and enthusiasm. He did a happiness one-eighty. It turned out the first relationship was an Influence Type mismatch, for he was a left-sided Three and she was a left-sided Four. The new relationship was an exact Type match.

What if you and your significant other are more than a full Type away from one another (i.e., a One and a Three, a Two and a Four, or a One and a Four)? In that case, I have a question for you: How did you two ever get together in the first place? Rarely are people that mismatched ever attracted to one another beyond a first date. When people say things like, "He was a nice guy, but just not my type," they really mean, "He was a nice guy, but just not my Influence Type."

As you know, all products and services and their marketing exude a certain degree of SAF newness, either high or low. Begin taking that into consideration when buying gifts for people. A Type Two couple I know once received as a gift from a Type Four couple a set of coffee table coasters. They were country-styled coasters with a duck design, something the Twos wouldn't be caught dead displaying in their home. I also saw a Type Four couple receive from a Type Two couple an equally mismatched gift. It was a set of sleek, avant-garde candlestick holders that came close to causing the Fours to gag as they pulled them out of the box. I'll bet you have some gift that comes out of the closet and sits on the coffee table only when the giver is scheduled to visit.

A friend of mine said he wouldn't be caught dead in a pair of Levi's Dockers. Even though he's 36, and in the bullseye of the product's target as far as age is concerned, his Influence Type does not match with the SAF newness Dockers advertising exudes. While he's on the left side of the Type Three range, the Dockers ads and commercials appeal to men on the right side of the Three range and all of the Four range. What did his sister give him for Christmas? (It could have been worse, he said. She could have given him two pairs.) His sister is a Four and so is her husband. The husband wears Dockers all the time and thinks they're wonderful.

Instead of giving a gift that you would be proud to use and display, give a gift the recipient would be feel comfortable with.

Use your knowledge of the SAF Factor and Influence Type to match item with person.

If you're ready to try an experiment, dress like an Influence Type other than your true Type the next time you attend a social gathering among friends. Usually slight adjustments in wardrobe are all you'll need. I guarantee you the people that are of the same Influence Type as your dress that day will say things like, "I haven't seen you wear that sweater before... it looks great on you!" and, "You know, I don't believe I've ever seen you look this good before!"

PLOT IT ON THE INFLUENCE GRAPH

Time to get back to work. Before we move to the next chapter, in which you'll learn a number of specific Influence Graph techniques for high-level demand creation, I want you to go through a short exercise.

I'm going to list a few particular brands of products and services, along with the Influence Type range they appeal to. As you read each item, see if you can identify the appeal range before looking at the answer. If you're close on most of them, you've got a good feel for matching SAF newness and Influence Type. If you're way off base, please re-read this chapter before moving on.*

Item	*Influence Type Appeal Range*
Ford Taurus	Three, Four
Nissan Maxima	One, Two
"Twin Peaks"	One, Two
"Matlock"	Half of Three, Four
Barry Manilow	Half of Three, Four
Madonna	One, Two, Three, Four
George Michael	Half of Two, Three, Four

---

*Note: Appeal ranges don't always start and end on the dividing line between Influence Types. They can start and end in the middle of the Types as well.

Michael Jackson	Two, Three, Four
INXS	Half of One, Two, Three
Absolut Vodka	One, Two, Three
Smirnoff Vodka	Three, Four
Budweiser	Three, Four
Bud Light	One, Two, Half of Three
Gallo	Three, Half of Four
Levi's 501 Jeans	One, Two
Levi's 505 Jeans	Half of Two, Three
Levi's Dockers	Half of Three, Four
Magnavox	Three, Four
Sony	One, Two, Half of Three
GQ	Half of One, Two, Half of Three
Cosmopolitan	Two, Three
Good Housekeeping	Half of Three, Four
Rolling Stone	One, Two, Half of three
Spin	One, Two
Maybelline	Half of Three, Four
Christian Dior (the cosmetics line)	One, Two
Erno Laszlo	One, Half of Two
Mary Kay	Half of Three, Four
Radio Shack	Three, Four
Sharper Image	One, Two
Benson & Hedges	Half of One, Two
Marlboro	Three, Four
Sears	Half of Three, Four
J.C. Penney	Half of Two, Three, Four
Bloomingdales	Half of One, Two, Half of Three
MTV	Two, Three
VH-1	Half of Two, Three, Half of Four
A&E	One, Half of Two
Häagen-Dazs	One, Two, Three
Sealtest	Half of Three, Four
Ritz Crackers	Three, Four
McCormick Crackers	One, Two

Chapter Sixteen

Putting the Combined Forces of Human Influence and Marketing to Work for You

H uman influence spreads via person-to-person contact. Relatives, friends, family members, acquaintances, co-workers, even strangers on the street are influencing one another all the time. When certain people buy and use your product or service, they are influencing others to do likewise.

Your marketing can cause human influence to flow. Through the correct application of certain marketing techniques, you not only can spur sales, but also you can spur adoptive human influence. And once you get the combined forces of human influence and your marketing working in harmony, your demand can mushroom to much greater heights than it otherwise would (this is one case in which synergy really happens).

In this chapter, you'll learn specific techniques that you can use to perform all sorts of marketing feats, like accurately predicting marketplace acceptance of a product or service before it's launched and spreading demand widely by keeping your product's or service's appeal alive in multiple Influence Types at the same time. You'll also learn how to create negative human influence, which can cause people to shun a competitor. And more.

The tool you will use to do all of this is The Influence Graph (if it's been a while since you read the last chapter, you may wish to familiarize yourself with The Influence Graph as shown in Figure 2, page 163). Your knowledge of SAF newness and Influence Types will also come into play. All these things work together.

Putting these Influence Graph techniques into operation involves a high level of marketing sophistication. But since you've made it through the first 15 chapters, I now declare you ready for advancement. It'll be fun, and well worth your effort.

Incidentally, in this chapter we'll talk about targeting different types of people according to Influence Type. In Chapter 11 we talked about targeting in terms of core and fringe. The two concepts are not contradictory; they are just different sides of the same coin. While the core and fringe deal mainly with the demographic side of targeting, Influence Types deal with the psychographic side. You should use both concepts together, not just one or the other.

HOW TO PREDICT MARKETPLACE ACCEPTANCE OF A NEW PRODUCT OR SERVICE

Gauging acceptance of a new product or service before it's launched can save you a lot of time, money, and grief. Many marketers seem to rely on the trial-and-error method quite often, which is definitely the hard way. Others rely on test marketing, which does have its advantages at times. But a much easier method is available to you, utilizing the knowledge you now possess. Simply determine how well your SAF newness matches your desired Influence Type. We talked about matching the two in the last chapter. The exercise you performed at the end of the chapter was designed to sharpen your matching skill. Notice that you ascertained the appeal range of each item on The Influence Graph through observation. You observed the level of SAF newness for each product or service and its marketing, then determined what Influence Type(s) would be most attracted.

You can also gauge the potential magnitude of your initial sales by knowing which Influence Types(s) you will attract. Remember, Ones represent 10 percent of the population, Twos 20 percent, Threes 40 percent, and Fours 30 percent. If your product or service appeals to Twos initially, your sales will be less than if it appeals to either Threes or Fours, but more than if it appealed only to Ones. Remember also that influence only moves to the right, never to the left. Targeting Ones or Twos initially might yield lower sales, but might grow into substantially more sales in time as adoptive influence moves into the Types to the right.

Match the SAF newness of your new product or service with the Influence Type(s) it will appeal to before you launch. If you don't like what you see, make adjustments in your SAF newness to suit.

Let's look at an example of what can happen when you fail to perform this exercise beforehand. One of ABC's new shows in the fall of 1990 was a drama called "Cop Rock." It was an innovative show from producer Steven Bochco ("St. Elsewhere," "L.A. Law," and "Doogie Howser, M.D." are some of his other shows). "Cop Rock" was actually a musical drama, in which actors would burst into song at various times throughout the show. It was not too different in concept from movie or broadway musicals, but radically different from your typical television drama.

If an SAF-intensive item is radically different, to whom must it appeal to get quick acceptance? Type Ones mainly, and Type Twos secondarily, because they are very receptive to SAF newness. Type Threes and Fours, who are much slower to accept new SAF, will not accept something so radically different as "Cop Rock" until human influence finally reaches them. That may be some time down the road, if ever. "Cop Rock," by its radically different nature, entered the marketplace with no chance of initial acceptance by Type Threes and Fours (which, as you know, total 70 percent of the population).

But that's not necessarily the problem. Many successful products and services enter a market with only Type One or Two acceptance, then proceed to *grow* Types Three and Four acceptance as influence reaches them over time.

The problem with "Cop Rock" is that it didn't appeal to Type Ones or Twos either! It was radically different, but difference alone is not enough to gain One or Two acceptance. The differences must display a high level of SAF newness. That means taking on artsy, avant-garde, arcane qualities. In the case of a television show, that means liberal use of vivid colors, innovative cinematography, and esoteric, cutting-edge music. "Cop Rock" displayed none of that. For example, the show featured music by Mike Post and Randy Newman, two artists who appeal to Types Three and Four, not One and Two.

The bottom line: Types One and Two shunned "Cop Rock" because it wasn't hip, and Types Three and Four shunned it because it was too different for them to accept. In other words, "Cop Rock" didn't match up with any Influence Type. If you tried to plot it on The Influence Graph, you'd discover it falls nowhere. As you might expect, the ratings were anemic, and ABC cancelled "Cop Rock" after only a few episodes.

THE TARGET LEFT STRATEGY

The *Target Left Strategy* is an excellent way to mesh your marketing with human influence to produce a combined force much greater than either separate force. Here's how it works.

Determine which Influence Type range you primarily want to appeal to from a sales standpoint. In other words, identify the Type range you want to buy your product now and in the future. Then shift your marketing target to the left of this range. The rule of thumb is this: Shift one-half an Influence Type to the left. For instance, if your sales target is primarily Type Threes, your marketing target will be the half-of-Two through half-of-Three range. This is depicted in Figure 3.

By shifting your marketing target to the left of your sales target, two advantages occur.

First, human influence works for you throughout your entire sales target range. Say your sales target is Type Three. By shifting your marketing target to the left, you initiate adoption in the right

FIGURE 3
The Influence Graph

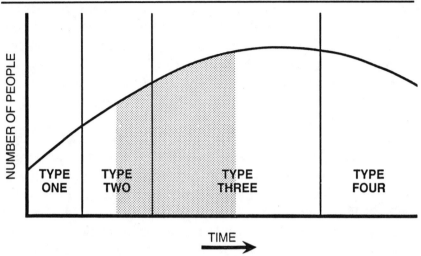

The shaded area is the optimum marketing target to affect Type Three individuals.

side of the Two range. These right-sided Twos then influence the left-sided Threes.

If, on the other hand, you do not shift your marketing target to the left and instead target the entire Three range straight on, the people on the left side of the Three range won't see the people to the left of them, the Twos, adopting. Adoptive human influence won't be affecting left-sided Threes. This result will be very unfortunate for you, since the people on the left side of your sales target exert a major influence on the people to the right of them.

Second, as you use the Target Left Strategy, you widen your potential buying universe to include some people to the left of your actual sales target. Remember, influence travels only to the right. Influence will never travel to the left of your target range. If you target only Threes, Threes and Fours are all you can potentially get. But when you include the right side of Two in your target, you can potentially get half of Two, Three, and Four.

Examples of the Target Left Strategy

Absolut is the number one selling brand of imported vodka in the United States. To sell as much as it does, it needs, and gets, acceptance throughout more than one Influence Type. Absolut's appeal range is Types One, Two, and Three. Yet Absolut targets its marketing to the left of this range. It targets Types One and Two (more than the standard half-Type shift, but effective nonetheless).

Here's another way of looking at it. Who influences the Threes to drink Absolut? Why, it's the Twos that do that. And who influences the Twos? The Ones do. By targeting to the range beginning with Type One and extending through Type Two, and letting the natural flow of human influence take care of the Three range, they end up with major Type Three acceptance. Adoptive influence steamrolls throughout the Type Three range on the impetus of previous adoption in the Types One and Two ranges.

Ralph Lauren's Polo brand of men's clothing also targets its marketing slightly to the left of its sales target. Polo's sales target is mainly Type Threes. Its marketing target is the half-of-Two through half-of-Three range (Figure 3, page 181).

Recall the rule of thumb for determining how far left to shift your marketing target: Target your marketing to a range that begins and ends one-half an Influence Type to the left of your primary sales target. For example, if your primary sales target is Type Threes, target your marketing half-a-notch to the left. Figure 3, shows the optimum marketing target to affect Type Three individuals.

By employing the Target Left Strategy, you're encouraging adoption to start farther to the left, which not only yields wider appeal (and greater sales), but also gets the power and momentum of human influence working throughout your entire sales target range.

Implementation Examples

Just how does Absolut go about targeting the One through Two range? By exuding a very high level of SAF newness in *some* of its marketing, starting with its package. It has a very unusual-looking bottle, with an uncommonly short neck. Absolut appeals to Ones and Twos promotionally by sponsoring art exhibits around the country. Some of the Absolut ads employ lots of subtlety and artistry. It uses media outlets that have mainly Types One and Two appeal for these high SAF newness ads, such as *Art & Antiques* and *Interview* magazines.

Absolut also prepares some ads with slightly less SAF newness and runs them in magazines with strong Type Two appeal (and which some Threes also see) such as *Rolling Stone, GQ,* and *Forbes.* Thus it has covered both ends of its One through Two marketing target range. (Hard liquors mainly use magazines due to legal restrictions regarding other media. Liquor advertising is prohibited by federal law on radio and television, and some local ordinances prohibit liquor advertising on billboards.)

Notice that Absolut adjusts the level of SAF newness in its ads based on the appeal of the media outlets it runs them in. This is very important. If you fail to produce different ads with varying levels of SAF newness for different media outlets with different Type appeal, you're mismatching SAF newness with Influence Type. That sets off the discomfort button in people who see your ad that mismatches their Influence Type. They get the feeling your product or service is not for them. If there were a seventh waste of marketing money, this would be it.

HOW TO SPREAD DEMAND QUICKLY WHEN LAUNCHING A NEW PRODUCT OR SERVICE

The Target Left Strategy works well either for an existing product or service or for a new one you are about to launch. In the case of a new product or service, however, some additional considerations come into play.

Immediately following the launch of a new product or service, it's highly unlikely that all the people in your marketing (or sales) target will instantly embrace your new item. More likely, the people on the left portion of your marketing target will initially adopt, but those on the right of your target range may delay adoption until human influence reaches them. Such is the nature of us humans.

You can, however, cause your adoptive influence to spread faster than it otherwise would by increasing the *awareness of adoption* that exists in the marketplace. People are influenced to adopt something when they become aware of someone slightly to the left of them adopting. But people don't see or hear about everything that other people buy and use. You may have recently purchased a new pair of running shoes, but since I see you only at the office, I've never seen you wearing them. Likewise, I may just have purchased a new vacuum cleaner, but when you come to visit it's away in the closet, out of sight, and I don't happen to mention it. Perhaps the product or service you just launched is not something every buyer will carry with him in full view wherever he goes; perhaps he won't run out in the street and shout to all his neighbors about the purchase.

When awareness of adoption is low, influence travels slower. When awareness of adoption is high, influence travels faster. If you want to speed things up, you must raise the awareness of adoption of your product or service. You do that through a technique called *simulated adoption.*

I said earlier that human influence flows via person-to-person contact, that is, one person adopting a particular behavior and in turn influencing others to do the same. You can stimulate this adoption through your marketing. You do that by creating ads and/or commercials which show certain Influence Types adopting your product or service and then exposing these ads and commercials to the next Influence Type to the right. This simulated adoption, which reaches people through exposure to your advertising, acts in concert with actual adoption, which reaches people through person-to-person contact. This synchronized, two-pronged approach causes adoptive behavior to happen much more quickly.

Once your product or service has gained initial adoption by a particular Influence Type, it's time to simulate adoption in some or all of your subsequent ads or commercials. Show your initial Influence Type adopting, either actual consumers or actors. Expose these ads and commercials in media outlets which appeal to the next Influence Type in line.

In earlier chapters I advised you to depict people using your product or service in your advertising, the better to express certain emotions. But I never said what these people should *look like*. I never said what type of environment these people should be seen in. But now that you're familiar with Influence Types and SAF newness, you can use them to your advantage. Use people in your ads who typify the Influence Type that is currently buying your product or service; they're the ones who will influence the people to their right. For example, say you gained initial acceptance from Type Twos. You then prepare ads and/or commercials that depict Type Two adoption and run them in media outlets with a strong Type Three appeal. What you're really doing is nudging influence along, shepherding it from one Influence Type to the next.

HOW TO ELIMINATE A RESISTANCE BARRIER

Resistance barriers exist throughout The Influence Graph, in various locations for various products and services. A resistance barrier impedes the flow of adoptive human influence. People on the right of a resistance barrier are not adopting and are not likely to start adopting a particular product or service. I used the television show "Twin Peaks" and *GQ* magazine in earlier examples. For "Twin Peaks," the resistance barrier was on the line between the Type Two and Type Three ranges. For *GQ*, the resistance barrier is in the middle of the Type Three range.

Resistance barriers exist for one reason: The level of SAF newness exuded by a product or service and its marketing is just too high for people to the right of the resistance barrier to accept.

There's only one way to eliminate a resistance barrier. Reduce or soften your level of SAF newness, in both your product or service and its marketing. That sounds simple, but it's actually a major undertaking. Here's why. Incremental reductions in your SAF newness level tend to keep adoption moving through The Influence Graph. When a resistance barrier arises, however, it means major SAF adjustments, in both your product or service and its marketing, are required to keep influence moving.

But are you really sure you want to eliminate your resistance barrier? The major changes in your level of SAF newness required to do so would surely have an adverse effect on the people you're already appealing to. If, for example, your resistance barrier is located somewhere in the Types Three or Four ranges, the low level of SAF newness required to break through the barrier would repel Ones and Twos. Is that really what you want to happen?

In some cases, your answer may be yes. You may not care about driving away a lot of people to the left of your resistance barrier. The offsetting adoption by other people to the right of your resistance barrier may suit your wishes just fine.

But be careful. Sometimes you're better off with what you have than what you might get. Absolut isn't interested in eliminating its resistance barrier, which falls on the line between the Types Three and Four ranges. To do so would require them to change practically their entire marketing approach, from the package to the advertising. It takes a wise marketer to realize the grass isn't always greener on the other side of the resistance barrier.

CREATE GARGANTUAN APPEAL
THROUGH NEW-OLD BALANCE

I mentioned some products in the last chapter that manage to get and keep appeal in all four Influence Types at the same time. The examples I cited were Pepsi, Madonna, the movie *Batman*, Levi's, and McDonald's. How do they keep Types One and Two from shunning while Types Three and Four adopt? There is a little-known secret that enables some marketers to create true mass appeal. (I doubt all those who manage to pull it off even know how they do it. Some have undoubtedly stumbled upon the secret without full realization.)

The technique that breeds concurrent appeal throughout The Influence Graph is called *New-Old Balance*. To achieve a state of New-Old Balance, the marketer must provide an equal amount of SAF newness, which satisfies Types One and Two, and SAF sameness, which satisfies Types Three and Four. Let's go through some of our examples and see how New-Old Balance is achieved.

McDonald's is a pillar of stability. You can walk into any Mc-Donald's in the world and order a Big Mac, fries, and a Coke—the same items McDonald's has been serving for decades. A Big Mac from a Detroit McDonald's even looks and tastes the same as a Big Mac from a Miami, Los Angeles, Little Rock, or Tokyo Mc-Donald's. Each McDonald's store is clean, and each gives you good-tasting food fast. With McDonald's, you know what to expect. A high level of sameness is depicted in some of McDonald's ads and commercials. They show Types Three and Four patronizing. That degree of SAF sameness and tradition is very attractive to Type Three and Four individuals.

But wait. While McDonald's is maintaining a stronghold on tradition, it's also changing. Seemingly there's always a new food item on the menu. There's always a new promotion or contest going on. No two McDonald's stores are decorated alike. (One in New York has a grand piano in it. One in Richmond, near the airport, has an airplane in it). McDonald's experiments with different, adventurous, innovative architecture in its building designs. No single McDonald's ad or commercial runs for more than a few weeks; they're always changing. Some ads and commercials, showing Types One and Two patronizing, are done in a very artsy style. The degree of SAF newness that McDonald's perpetuates attracts Types One and Two and keeps them from shunning.

If there is anyone who knows how to work The Influence Graph, it's Madonna. She does it through an exquisite display of New-Old Balance. Almost every one of her songs is a simple pop ditty that everyone from seven to 70 can tap their feet to, sing along with, and enjoy. Her music requires practically no effort to understand and appreciate. Madonna's music has a low level of SAF newness, which appeals to Types Three and Four.

But wait. Every time another Madonna album comes out, her appearance is completely different. Madonna is constantly changing her look, never staying with one look more than a year or so. And for those people who do put forth an effort when listening to her songs, many artistic nuances can be found. (Lo and behold, the SAF newness is there after all. It just takes an effort to hear it.) Her videos are on the cutting-edge of artistic innovation. In fact, she often pushes the edge to its extreme. Madonna shows enough SAF newness for Types One and Two to justify their acceptance and override any shunning tendencies.

The Levi Strauss Company employs New-Old Balance in its own way. The quality, feel, and look of its denim jeans is the same as it's been for a hundred years. Conservative and traditional. A low level of SAF newness. Types Three and Four appeal.

But wait. Levi's made one little design alteration in its 501 jeans that punched tradition right in the mouth. It took out the zipper and replaced it with buttons. The ads and commercials for Levi's 501 jeans are very artsy and innovative. A high level of SAF newness. Types One and Two appeal. Although each particular line of pants, 501, 505, Dockers, and so on, has its own appeal range, the name Levi's is accepted by all Influence Types through New-Old Balance.

The *Batman* movie has a simple, easily understood plot that takes no effort to consume. The *Batman* character has also been around for over 50 years, yielding tremendous familiarity. Three and Four appeal. Yet the movie was directed by Tim Burton, known for his high degree of cinematic artistry and innovation, and Prince did the music. One and Two appeal.

You can employ New-Old Balance as well. It's a matter of keeping some aspects of your product or service and its marketing the same year after year, thus exuding a low level of SAF newness, and constantly changing other aspects of your product or service and its marketing, thus exuding a high level of SAF newness.

You don't have to be a large-scale marketer with deep pockets to utilize New-Old Balance. Any-sized marketer can do it once she knows how. Pleasants Hardware in Richmond, Virginia, plays up the fact that it's been in existence for over 75 years. Company advertising emphasizes the fact that Pleasants is a "time-honored tradition." Three and Four appeal. Yet its slogan is "The Great Big Toy Store for Adults," a somewhat off-the-wall slogan for a hardware store. The exterior of the store has a unique design that is updated regularly. The interior features classy burgundy carpeting, low ceilings with exposed air ducts painted cobalt blue, and interesting lighting arrangements. Remember, this is a hardware store, inherently SAF-light. But by boosting its level of SAF newness just enough, Type One and Two appeal results and augments its Three and Four appeal.

Through New-Old Balance, you're constantly feeding the demand fire by giving Types One and Two the SAF newness and innovation they're comfortable with. At the same time, you're achieving mass acceptance by giving Types Three and Four the sameness and stability they're comfortable with. When you've reached the apex of true New-Old Balance, you've created demand of gargantuan proportions. Break out the champagne.

A word of caution: You cannot achieve New-Old Balance by simply dividing up the SAF newness and sameness between your marketing and your product. Like keeping your product the same and putting all your SAF newness into your marketing. To gain real Type One and Two appeal, your product or service itself must have some element of newness or innovation. If Levi's 501 jeans didn't have the button fly, Ones and Twos wouldn't be buying no matter how artsy the commercials are. If Madonna's videos and concerts (which are part of her product) weren't on the edge, her changes in appearance wouldn't be enough to legitimize her as far as Ones and Twos are concerned, and they would have shunned her years ago.

INSTIGATE SHUNNING
THROUGH NEGATIVE INFLUENCE

As I've noted throughout this discussion, shunning occurs when people are influenced to stop a particular behavior or not to engage in it in the first place. In most cases, shunning is not something a marketer strives for, at least not for his own product or service.

But there are a couple instances in which you might want to instigate shunning. For one, you may wish to cause people to shun a competing product or service. For another, you may wish to cause a socially, morally, legally, or otherwise undesirable act, such as drug abuse or shoplifting, to subside.

Shunning is caused by *negative influence*. Up to this point, when I spoke of human influence, I was referring to positive human influence. That is, influence that persuades a person to adopt some type of behavior. But negative influence persuades a person to stop a certain type of behavior or never to begin adoption. You saw evidence of negative influence earlier when we discovered that Type Ones tend to shun certain products and services when they see Types Three and Four adopting.

How Negative Human Influence Works

People are positively influenced by others who are slightly to the left of themselves on The Influence Graph, that is, by people similar to themselves though slightly more receptive to SAF newness. People are negatively influenced by others unlike themselves, that is, by people who are one-and-a-half or two Influence Types away from them on The Influence Graph in either direction. In that sense, what is positive influence to some can be negative influence to others at the same time.

I emphasized earlier that there are no good or bad values attached to Influence Types. It's no better to be a Type One than it is to be a Type Two, Three, or Four. As a marketer, you must maintain this unbiased perspective when you identify people by Influence Type. But people themselves tend to view one another with bias. And the bias increases with Influence Type separation.

Type Fours, for instance, tend to view Type Ones as "weird" or "bizarre." When a Four sees a One adopting a particular product or service, the Four determines it's not for him. He has thus been negatively influenced. Type Ones tend to view Type Fours as "square" or "unhip." When a One sees a Four adopting some product or service, the One feels compelled to shun. The One has been negatively influenced.

Although less intense than the bias that exists between the polarized Ones and Fours, bias exists between other influence Types as well. Everyone, by the way, tends to view himself as "normal." As in George Carlin's bit about driving along the highway. If someone is driving faster than us he's a maniac, and if someone is driving slower than us he's an idiot. From our own perspective, we are always correct.

I pointed out earlier that a marketer could inadvertently nurture negative influence by using the wrong Influence Types in his advertising, for example, by showing Type Threes using your product when you're trying to get Type One adoption going. If you use human beings in your advertising, be aware of what Influence Type they appear to be.

Here are the procedures to instigate shunning:

- **Step 1: Determine what Influence Type you want to shun.** Let's say you want Type Twos to shun a competing soft drink, for example.

- **Step 2: Depict adoption by a non-adjacent Influence Type.** The non-adjacent Type to a Two is a Four (Types One and Three are adjacent to Type Two). Create an ad or commercial showing Fours adopting the competing soft drink.

  This is exactly what Pepsi did. A recent television commercial showed singer M. C. Hammer in concert singing one of his songs. The artist and song appeal to the half-of-Two through Three range. Well, someone switches his soft drink from Pepsi to Coke, and after inadvertently taking a swig of Coke, he suddenly bursts into "Feelings," an old Morris Albert tune from 1975, and a quintessential Four-appeal song. People in the audience can't figure out what's happened to M. C. (why he's turned into a Four) until someone offers him a Pepsi, and after drinking it he shifts back into his normal song. The message, directed to Twos and Threes: Coke is for people unlike you (Fours); Pepsi is for people like you (Twos and Threes).

  Note: You needn't necessarily mention competing brands by name to instigate shunning. References to types of products or services in a more generic fashion can be just as effective.

- **Step 3: Use media outlets or programs that appeal to the Type you want to shun.** You may not want everyone and anyone to be aware of your shun-instigating ads or commercials. Think what would happen if Type Fours saw Pepsi's M. C. Hammer commercial. They probably wouldn't get the intended message, since the song "Feelings" would not turn them off. The message they would get is that Pepsi is for people unlike themselves, and Coke is for them. This Pepsi commercial would actually strengthen Coke's appeal among Fours, not something Pepsi wants to happen (Pepsi wants as many people to drink Pepsi as possible, including Fours). That's why Pepsi runs this particular commercial in programs whose appeal drops off short of the Four range.

Chapter Seventeen

The Inattentive State: How People Receive Advertising

The question is not whether or not the public pays attention to advertising. We all know there is a serious lack of attention to ads and commercials. The real question is, "What can you, the marketer, do to circumvent the condition?"

I've run into very few marketers who know how to deal properly with the lack of attention their ads and commercials naturally engender. Although in every ad campaign strategy session there's always someone who stands up and excitedly declares, "But first we've got to get their attention!", I can assure you that "attention getting" is not the optimum solution to the problem. Your advertising must be effective whether people are paying attention or not, and I'm going to show you how.

In the next two chapters you will learn specific strategies and techniques to improve your advertising effectiveness tremendously in our attention-poor environment. But first we must step back and look at *how* people behave at the receiving end of advertising, and *why* so many people aren't paying attention in the first place.

THE ATTENTION DILEMMA

Let's say you have a television commercial currently running on a few stations or networks and a print ad running in a newspaper. How important is it to you that people pay attention to your commercial and ad? Does the effectiveness of your commercial and ad depend on whether or not people are paying attention to it? Most marketers feel the effectiveness of their advertising depends a great deal on the amount of attention it can garner. After all, if you don't have people's attention, you may as well be talking to the wall, right?

Your dilemma is, however, that only a small percentage of the people watching television any time your commercial airs, or flipping past your newspaper ad, will actually pay attention to it. (Lack of attention to advertising occurs in all media outlet types, not just television and newspapers. However, to keep our discussion from getting too unwieldy, I'll stick mainly with these two for now.) That's easy to understand. It's obvious that television viewers tune in to watch the programming content, not the commercial content. Likewise, the newspaper reader seeks news, not advertisements.

It's interesting to observe people as they watch television or read a newspaper. Here's an experiment I'd like you to try. Watch what television viewers do when a commercial comes on. Chances are, they will turn their heads away from the television and look about the room. They'll engage in some other activity, such as picking up some reading material, letting the dog out, looking out the window, or visiting the bathroom or kitchen. When a commercial break comes on, you can literally see attention turning away from the television. And that doesn't include the people who still watch the screen and may appear to be paying attention, but whose minds wander elsewhere.

Next time you're watching a television program with other people in the room, see how long it takes for someone to begin speaking when a commercial comes on. People have been conditioned to converse with one another during commercial breaks. It never fails. I will bet you someone in the room will begin speaking within five seconds from when the first commercial begins, every time. ("Zapping," when viewers grab the remote control and change the channel during a commercial break, is another matter altogether. I'm not addressing that issue. This discussion deals with the people who are at least exposed to a commercial, yet do not pay attention to it.)

The point is, you want people to pay attention to your ads or commercials, but most people don't. Another way of saying it is that people are not receiving your ad or commercial in the attentive manner you have intended. Either way you look at it, the lack of attention by the audience causes your advertising to suffer a significant loss of impact.

TWENTY PERCENT IS ALL YOU GET

Just what percentage of people who are exposed to the average ad or commercial pay conscious attention to it? That is a difficult question to answer. If we piece together all the research available, including the results of a study recently completed by my own firm, we can conclude that roughly 20 percent—one person out of five—is consciously paying attention to the average ad or commercial each time they're exposed to it. That means 80 percent of the people are not paying conscious attention to an ad or commercial each time they're exposed to it.

Does that surprise you? Most industry professionals in advertising and marketing that I've mentioned this 20 percent figure to are surprised it's that high. Most guess the attention level would be closer to 10 percent.

(Don't get bogged down debating the numbers. A highly accurate, scientifically valid figure is probably impossible to obtain and isn't really necessary. A 20 percent attention level is in the ballpark, and is a good working number for our purposes.)

INTRODUCTION TO INATTENTION

Most of the time people simply do not pay conscious attention to advertising. Not because so many ads and commercials are too esoteric or above their head; they're not. Not because so many ads and commercials are poorly produced; they're not. But because most people are predisposed to divert their attention elsewhere, regardless of all those other factors. With regard to advertising, *people don't want to pay attention.* It's as simple as that.

We call the lack of attention *inattention.* When the brain drops into a state of inattention with regard to the matter in question, that person is said to be in an *inattentive state.* Have you ever driven past the freeway exit you intended to use? With regard to your driving, you were in an inattentive state. At the same time, you were probably in an *attentive state* with regard to something else... talking to a passenger or thinking about a problem, perhaps. Have you ever found yourself mentally "tuning out" while your spouse or child was speaking to you? With regard to the other person's speaking, your brain was in an inattentive state, although you may have been in an attentive state with regard to something else at the time.

WHY INATTENTION OCCURS

People have learned to go into a state of inattention when an ad or commercial reaches their brain. There are three main reasons why this programmed inattention exists.

1. Ever since the advent of radio and television, broadcasters have conditioned the public to treat a commercial mentally as a "break" or "interruption" in the programming. Phrases like, "Now a word from our sponsor," "We'll be back after this message," and "When we return" tell the viewer or listener to divert his attention. (Once conditioned, the viewer needn't hear those types of phrases to go into an inattentive state. The appearance of the first commercial in the break will most often trigger the state.)

    With newspapers and magazines, the inattentive state with respect to ads is programmed into the reader's mind for exactly the opposite reason. Most newspapers and magazines intentionally ignore that they have ads in them. By so doing they condition the reader to ignore the ads as well.

Say you're reading an article on page D3 and at the bottom of the page it says, "Continued on page D17." So you flip to D17 and continue reading. The fact that there were 14 pages in between D3 and D17, containing numerous ads, was never mentioned. Should the newspaper have said, "Please read the ads on pages D4 through D16 before going to the remainder of this article on page D17"?

Before you blame the media for causing inattention, realize that no other alternative is really feasible. The distinct separation of program and/or editorial content and commercial content is desirable for reasons other than those of interest to the marketer. It goes back to some of the principles upon which this country was founded, including the freedom of speech and independence of thought. Newspapers and news broadcasts (collectively referred to as "the press") would not be able to maintain integrity and responsibility to the public if they bowed to commercial interests.

However, marketers have devised ways to blur the lines between program/editorial content and their ads over the years anyway. Have you ever seen a newspaper ad, for example, that looked just like a news story in wording and design? The newspaper requires that the word "Advertisement" appear at the top of the ad to distinguish it, but the marketer is hoping you don't notice that word.

Recently, marketers have raised eyebrows with so-called "infomercials," which are program-length (30- or 60-minute) television commercials in the guise of a program. Marketers also pay movie studios thousands just to have their particular product show up in a scene or two. The blending of program and commercial content is intended partially to circumvent inattention.

2. Inattention exists with reference to advertisements because of a mental function called *state default*. Inattention is a relaxed state which normally dominates unless it is overridden by a more powerful stimulus. In the absence of overriding stimuli, the brain defaults into the inattentive state. Since advertising is not important to most people, their brains assign it a very low value. A value that usually

is not strong enough to switch the mind into an attentive state when exposed to an ad or commercial.

3. People consciously plan to divert their attention in the first place. Have you ever had the television or radio on even though you were consciously paying attention to something else . . . cleaning the house, playing cards, or eating a meal, perhaps? "Wallpaper video," when the television is on but no one is consciously watching, is becoming more commonplace. And radio has been used as "background" for years. Sometimes we "read" a newspaper simply by flipping through the pages in rapid succession, stopping only to absorb a headline or two along the way. In these cases, the viewer, listener, or reader is in the inattentive state with regard to the entire thing—program/editorial content and commercial content combined.

HOW DO YOU HANDLE INATTENTION?

As incredible as it may seem, many marketers do nothing about the fact that the majority of the people they're paying to reach through the media are not paying attention to their advertising. Even when they acknowledge the lack of attention, they usually ignore it. Some marketers want to believe that people *are* paying attention to their ads and commercials, despite any amount of evidence to the contrary. Ad agencies and media outlets tend to reinforce this belief. To do otherwise—to acknowledge any weakness in the system—would be committing professional suicide. What agency, after all, will tell a client it's produced a wonderful television commercial that most people are not going to pay attention to? And what network or station would dare point out that the majority of its viewers are paying attention to the programs but not the commercials?

Consequently, some marketers function as though everything they do will have a major impact—that people will hang on every word of ad copy and respond accordingly. These marketers are always the ones who suffer from chronic disappointment and frustration with the ensuing results, nevertheless they plod on. You might expect such a marketer to awaken eventually and recognize reality. Many do. Yet you can look over the vast field of active marketers at any time and still see half of them with their heads in the sand.

Many other marketers do address the problem of inattention, however. In so doing, they usually end up implementing one or both of the following strategies. Let's examine each and see just how effective they really are.

The Bang Away Strategy

If only one person out of five is paying conscious attention to an ad or commercial each time it runs, why not run the ad or commercial five times and thereby catch everyone in the attentive state at least once? There's no reason why not. The practice of using multiple exposures, or "frequency," is an integral part of advertising. The concept is as old as advertising itself. In fact, if you're not running your ads and commercials with healthy frequency, chances are you're falling short of the results threshold.

I'll assume that you, as the no-wet-behind-the-ears marketer that you are, are already running your ads and commercials with proper frequency. How do you increase their effectiveness even further? Do you simply increase the frequency even further?

Remember, higher frequency equals higher effectiveness . . . to a point. The point of diminishing returns, at which additional exposures produce little if any additional result, actually sets in rather quickly.* Yet some marketers behave as though effectiveness keeps increasing the more they bang away.

In some cases, increased frequency not only produces no additional effectiveness, but actually *decreases* effectiveness. Haven't you ever noticed an ad or commercial that you've seen so many times it becomes a major annoyance? You're consciously aware of it, all right; and you're ready to zap the television, punch the radio, or throw down the newspaper the next time you see or hear it. "Will someone please tell these

---

*For a definitive and technical explanation, read *Effective Frequency: The Relationship Between Frequency and Advertising Effectiveness* by Michael J. Naples (Association of National Advertisers, Inc., 1979.)

marketers to back off?" you plead. (Contrary to what some may believe, all awareness is not good awareness.)

Most marketers who implement the *Bang Away Strategy* at one time or another eventually give up on it. One can spend only so much money before the lack of acceptable return forces one to do otherwise.

The Clutter Buster Strategy

In the early 80s, the *Clutter Buster Strategy* developed. The idea is to attract attention by having your ad or commercial jump out from all the others which surround it. In television, for example, your commercial must somehow "bust through the clutter" to be noticed, the "clutter" being all the other commercials on the air. In other words, every advertiser views every other advertiser's commercials as part of the clutter. In the eyes of other advertisers, *your* commercial is part of the clutter. How do you like that?!

The Clutter Buster Strategy has resulted in an improvement in the overall quality of commercials and ads, no doubt. But since every marketer is trying to break through the clutter of every other marketer's ads and commercials, the net result is close to zero. Like all the runners in a pack deciding to pour on a burst of speed at once to break out, the entire pack moves faster, but it's still a pack.

In the 90s and beyond, a high quality ad or commercial is essential *to keep from dropping back of the pack* rather than to forge ahead of it.

THE REAL ANSWER

If the Bang Away Strategy and the Clutter Buster Strategy come up short, what is the answer? How do you increase the level of attention to your ads and commercials?

Would you believe the answer to increasing the effectiveness of your advertising is *not* to increase the level of attention to your ads above that which it naturally garners? If you think I'm kidding, consider this: *People do not want your ad or commercial to kick them into attention.* They're perfectly happy being in the inattentive state when they see or hear your ad or commercial. In fact, all people, you and I included, have an instinctive defense mechanism in place to keep the majority of ads and commercials from getting our conscious attention.

Therefore, if you're trying constantly to get people's attention, you're fighting the natural desires of the consumer. It's like a tug of war you've got going. You're pulling in one direction, the consumer is pulling in the other. One of the tenets upon which this book is based is that the marketer can achieve the highest level of success only by catering to the inmost needs and desires of the consumer. Fighting the consumer is not the answer to creating major demand. The real answer to incredible advertising impact, in which the marketer and consumer work together, is the subject of the next chapter. Meet you there.

Chapter Eighteen

The Simulconscious Strategy

H ere's the good news you've been waiting for: *It doesn't matter whether people are paying attention to your advertising or not. You can increase the effectiveness of your advertising significantly even when the majority of people that are exposed to it are in the inattentive state.* The idea is to program your commercial for people in the inattentive state as well as for those in the attentive state. It's called the *Simulconscious Strategy*. The process itself is called *simulconsciousing*.

When you implement the Simulconscious Strategy, you actually design your commercial to penetrate and impress the conscious mind (which takes care of those in the attentive state), and the subconscious mind (which affects those in the inattentive state). And you do both simultaneously.

HOW SIMULCONSCIOUSING WORKS

Preparing your message for people in the attentive state is easy. That's what you're already doing. Preparing your commercial for people in the inattentive state is not any more difficult, but it is different. It may even seem a bit awkward at first.

When you program your ad or commercial for inattentive reception, you're introducing certain elements which penetrate the subconscious mind and make subconscious impressions. Affecting the subconscious mind is important because (*a*) most often it is the subconscious mind that controls want and desire (remember the power-wants are deeply subconscious), and (*b*) subconscious impressions create top-of-mind awareness, itself an important factor in demand creation. Making numerous, on-going subconscious impressions is one of the most important parts of demand creation.

Here's the real beauty of it: People in the inattentive state are only inattentive on the conscious level. Their subconscious minds remain wide open for impression in the inattentive state.

When you are simulconsciousing, you prepare your ad or commercial in such a manner as to penetrate and impress the conscious as well as the subconscious minds. Therefore, an impression is made regardless of which state—attentive or inattentive—a person is in at the time of exposure.

HOW A SIMULCONSCIOUS COMMERCIAL IS RECEIVED

Consider what happens at the receiving end of a television commercial, starting with a regular, non-simulconsciously constructed commercial. An attentive viewer will consciously see whatever appears on the screen and hear whatever is contained on the audio track. I'm not saying such a person is *studying* the commercial and detecting every detail. I'm saying an attentive viewer is paying just enough attention to be consciously aware of the commercial and get the gist of the message.

But the conscious mind of the inattentive viewer is not on the commercial. His conscious mind is focused on something else... a conversation he is having with another person in the room, let's say. Although that person's eyes cross the television screen once or twice while the commercial is running and the person's ears can still hear the audio portion, *the message does not register; it makes no impact.* For the inattentive viewer, the commercial *doesn't even exist.*

Why not? Because no material with the ability to penetrate and affect the subconscious mind was contained in the commercial.

Only material that could reach and affect the conscious mind was presented, and the inattentive viewer does not give the commercial the conscious attention required to receive it.

Now look what happens in the case of a simulconsciously constructed commercial. For the attentive viewer, the commercial probably appears no different from the non-simulconsciously constructed commercial. That is, the differences are not very noticeable. The attentive viewer, you'll recall, is not studying the commercial, only paying nominal attention. She pays enough attention to get the gist of the message of the non-simulconscious commercial, and she pays enough attention to get the gist of the simulconscious commercial, without much difference resulting either way. (Attentive viewers who *are* inclined to study the commercial, such as professional advertising and marketing people, would notice distinct differences between the simulconscious and the non-simulconscious versions. To name the differences now would be to get ahead of myself. We'll get into the specifics in a minute.)

The inattentive viewer, on the other hand, is not aware of the commercial on the conscious level, which is no different from what occurs with the non-simulconscious version. But here's where things begin to differ greatly. As the inattentive viewer's eyes cross the television screen a couple times during the simulconsciously constructed commercial and his or her ears receive the audio portion, *certain material from both the video and audio penetrate the subconscious and make valuable subconscious impressions.* Why? Because the commercial was *prepared to be received on the subconscious level* as well as on the conscious level. That's what the Simulconscious Strategy is all about. You program your advertising with information which registers not only consciously but subconsciously as well. This will become clearer to you as you read the remainder of this chapter and the next.

Simulconsciousing Is Not Subliminal Perception

Do not confuse simulconsciousing with subliminal perception. The two are completely different and have nothing to do with one another. Here's how they differ.

When you program a message for subliminal perception, you specifically design it to bypass the conscious mind entirely and go straight to the subconscious. For example, perhaps you've heard one of those subliminal self-improvement tapes which everyone and his uncle is marketing these days. All you consciously hear is music or ocean waves. The actual behavior-influencing message is at an inaudible level and can be detected only by your subconscious mind. The message has been prepared for perception by the subconscious mind only.

With the Simulconscious Strategy, you do not attempt to bypass the conscious mind at all. There are no "subliminal messages" which the receiver cannot consciously detect. Unlike messages designed for subliminal perception, which pre-determines they will be received strictly on the subconscious level, simulconsciousing does not pre-determine at which level of consciousness they will be received. Rather, each person receiving the message determines how he or she will receive the message—consciously or subconsciously—based on whether he or she is in the attentive or inattentive state at the time.

Have you ever caught yourself humming or singing a particular song, either in your mind or out loud, at a time when you were not actually hearing the song? You probably heard the song on the radio or somewhere else hours or days earlier, but you don't remember hearing it. You were in the inattentive state at the time you heard it, yet it registered nonetheless, and here you are humming it some time later. The song was not some subliminal piece of information. It was perfectly audible on the conscious level, even though you weren't listening to it on the conscious level. Songs with strong "hooks" are simulconscious gems. The idea is to make your ads and commercials work the same way.

THE SIMULCONSCIOUS AD ELEMENTS

As you'll recall from our discussion of pre-processing in Chapter 10, only certain pieces of information can penetrate the subconscious mind and make an instant impression. All the other stuff— the vast amount of information the subconscious mind receives but cannot handle without sending it to the conscious mind for processing—makes no impact most of the time.

There are three pieces of information which are powerful enough to make subconscious impressions on people in the inattentive state. We call them the *simulconscious ad elements*. When you are simulconsciousing, you include the simulconscious ad elements in your ad or commercial in a specific manner.

The first simulconscious ad element is your pre-processed word. The second element is your brand name or logo. Both of these were discussed in Chapter 10. The third element is your *point line*, which we'll discuss now.

A point line is a one-sentence explanation or summary of what you're trying to get across in your ad or commercial. It is, simply, the point. How do you create a point line? Imagine someone who is exposed to your ad or commercial anxiously shouting to you, "What are you trying to tell me here? I don't have the time or energy to devote to your commercial, so just give me the point! What is the point?!" Your answer, delivered as succinctly as possible, is your point line.

A point line is not necessarily the same thing as a slogan, although the two can be one and the same in certain instances. Slogans most often make a point about the company as opposed to a specific product. They also tend to be image-oriented, rather than about a specific offer. A point line, on the other hand, summarizes the specific message in the ad or commercial in which it appears. For example, say AT&T produces a television commercial emphasizing the small and insignificant savings one realizes with competing long-distance companies (I'm not taking sides in the long-distance war, merely putting myself in the shoes of AT&T for the moment). The commercial's point line might be, "You save just as much with AT&T." Their slogan, on the other hand, is "The Right Choice."

State Farm has some ads and commercials with a point line that says, "State Farm sells life insurance." Straight and simple. Wendy's current slogan is, "The Best Hamburgers And A Whole Lot More," but the point line of a particular commercial which introduces a new grilled chicken sandwich might be, "Try our new grilled chicken sandwich." Remember, a point line is the essence of a particular ad or commercial. The simpler and more straightforward, the better.

THE RESULTS OF SIMULCONSCIOUSING

Of those in the inattentive state who receive exposure to your advertising, the simulconscious ad elements (pre-processed word, logo, and point line) are all that will penetrate their minds. And sometimes not all three elements will make it. Although your pre-processed word and attached logo or name make an impression virtually 100 percent of the time a person sees or hears them, your point line will make an impression only about half the time.

What little, insignificant impression you may think you are making actually has a cumulative effect that builds up within the subconscious mind to a highly potent level after only a few such impressions. That's why it's very important to program your ads for the subconscious as well as the conscious mind at all times. The results you receive from implementing the Simulconscious Strategy can be dramatic. And they can begin to happen soon after implementation!

EXACTLY HOW DO YOU DO SIMULCONSCIOUSING?

How you integrate the simulconscious ad elements into the conscious material in each of your ads or commercials is critical. The *form* in which the three simulconscious ad elements appear in your ads and commercials is as important as the elements themselves. Because the optimum form varies depending on medium, we'll discuss precisely how to construct your advertising using the Simulconscious Strategy for specific mediums in the next chapter.

Chapter Nineteen

How to Double the Effectiveness of Your Advertising at No Additional Cost

O kay, you've flipped ahead to this chapter to find out what in the world could possibly double your advertising's effectiveness at no cost. I won't keep you waiting. The secret is to use the Simulconscious Strategy. It's the integration of the simulconscious ad elements—your pre-processed word, logo, and point line—into your ads and commercials in a specific manner.

Readers who have reached this chapter by way of the preceding 18 chapters are entitled to smirk. They know you have no idea what I'm talking about. You see, this whole demand creation business, including the doubling of your advertising's effectiveness, is a building process. Each successive move you make builds upon your previous moves. In other words, you've got to read and implement what I've presented in the preceding 18 chapters before you'll be ready to do any effectiveness doubling. This chapter will still be here when you get back.

For those who are ready, let's begin.

When your ad or commercial is properly simulconscioused, it affects people who are paying attention to it—those in the attentive state—and it affects people who are not paying attention to it—those in the inattentive state. Compared to a non-simulcon-scioused ad or commercial, which affects only those in the attentive state, your simulconscioused ad or commercial is twice as effective.

Actually, the effectiveness of your advertising may more than double. Since 80 percent of the receivers of each ad or commercial are in the inattentive state, you really have the potential of tripling, quadrupling, or quintupling your effectiveness when you start affecting these people. But let's be very conservative and say we have a high degree of confidence that the effectiveness of our advertising will at least double when we are simulconscious-ing.

As for the cost, that stays the same. It costs you no more to simulconscious your ads or commercials, from either a production or media buying standpoint.

One more thing before we begin. As is the case with every strategy and technique in this book, simulconsciousing works for both the small-scale marketer and the large-scale marketer. Whether you're a one-person entrepreneur with a smallish ad in the weekly shopper or one of the nation's top advertisers, simulconsciousing will work for you. I point this out to keep you from getting the impression simulconsciousing is meant for marketers unlike yourself. It's for *you*.

HOW TO SIMULCONSCIOUS YOUR TELEVISION COMMERCIALS

Simulconsciously constructing your television commercials does not mean you must alter their concept, theme, or storyline from what they would otherwise be. Integrating the simulconscious ad elements into your commercials won't displace any other elements in the commercials. For the most part, things remain intact.

However, incorporating your simulconscious ad elements will alter the way your commercial looks and sounds. Its style and format will be affected. Here is the specific procedure to simul-conscious your commercials.

- **Step 1: Begin your commercial with your pre-processed word and logo.** Your pre-processed word and logo should appear at the same time. They should be on the screen the first $1\frac{1}{2}$ seconds of your commercial.

Here's an example. In a McDonald's McRib commercial, airing in late 1990, the McDonald's logo appeared for the first second or two in the lower right hand corner of the screen, superimposed over the scene of a family looking hungry and displaying excitement. Then the word "Hungry?" was superimposed over the action. Although it would have been better to show the pre-processed word "Hungry?" and the McDonald's logo at the same time, instead of one following the other, this is as close to perfect an example as one might presently find.

Your pre-processed word and logo needn't be the only things on the screen for the first $1\frac{1}{2}$ seconds. They can be superimposed over the action, as in this McDonald's commercial.

One of the biggest mistakes marketers make is to wait until the end of their commercial to show their logo, as though they feel compelled to make a statement first, then inform the viewer who made the statement. When you place a phone call to someone who may not know you or recognize your voice, do you begin making statements without first identifying yourself? I doubt it. If you refuse or neglect to identify yourself at the very outset of your conversation, the other person may become instantly annoyed. She may interrupt you and ask you to identify yourself, or she may even refuse to speak with you. Clearly, you do yourself no favors by withholding your name when initiating a phone conversation. Why then would you want to hold back your company or product name until the end in your television commercials? Are you afraid people will tune out if they realize it's you?

Here's why the first $1\frac{1}{2}$ seconds are the most critical portion of your commercial, and why your logo needs to be on the screen then. That is the time when the viewer's brain is most receptive to influence, even in the inattentive state. That is the time when the brain actually lowers its defenses and welcomes information. The brain uses the information it receives in the first $1\frac{1}{2}$ seconds to decide what state to assume, attentive or inattentive. Your logo makes its strongest possible impact during this brief window of welcome.

Hey! If this is true, if the viewer uses the first $1\frac{1}{2}$ seconds to help determine his state, why not present something that jolts the viewer into attention? There are two reasons why not. First, people have seen it all so many times before, they've become numb to whatever jolting information you might present. (The only two sure-fire attention-triggers left are the words "News Bulletin" and a naked person, neither of which you can likely use.)

Second, as I mentioned before, you're fighting the viewer when your main objective is to jolt him to attention. The viewer doesn't want to pay attention most of the time. What the viewer does want at the beginning of a commercial is an answer to the question, "Who is about to speak to me?" Give him the answer he seeks, and you will have a better chance to keep him around for whatever else you have to say.

- **Step 2: Show your logo repeatedly throughout your commercial.** Even in the inattentive state, a viewer's eyes cross the screen periodically. Although the brain is less receptive to information throughout a commercial than in the first $1\frac{1}{2}$ seconds, the brain will still register information it doesn't have to process. Your logo should appear many times throughout your commercial.

A recent Budweiser commercial is a good example. It starts with a close-up shot of the can, which, of course, shows the logo (showing your logo attached to your product is even better than showing it unattached to your product). Throughout the 30-second commercial, the Budweiser logo appears no fewer than six times, including once in huge letters as a crawl (when the word moves across the screen from right to left).

McDonald's does the same thing. You'll often see scenes of people eating in a McDonald's restaurant in which the people are sitting in front of a window with a huge "M" on it. And you see McDonald's bags and drink cups with the logo. McDonald's will often show an outside shot of the store, featuring the McDonald's sign.

Did you ever notice some television stations and cable channels superimposing their logos on the lower left- or right-hand portion of the screen periodically during programs? CNN and TBS do it. VH-1 goes one step further and leaves a "watermark" version of their logo on the screen all the time. The reason is not just to inform people what channel they are watching, it's to make a subconscious impression so viewers will better recall the channel when the rating services inquire.

What if it would appear awkward for your logo to pop up periodically throughout your commercial? Good! One of the ways to make your logo impress inattentive viewers is to let it "hang" or "fly" without any apparent physical or logical attachment to anything else going on. Don't feel your scenes need to contain some logical justification for a logo to be shown. Drop your logo in throughout your commercial in various ways, even if it appears awkward to you. After you do it a few times, it won't appear so awkward. Trust me.

- **Step 3: Deliver your point line right after one of your logo appearances.** Your point line needn't appear visually. Stating it in the audio track is fine. Just make sure it follows one of your logo appearances anywhere in your commercial (the logo may be visual, the point line auditory).

Your point line will affect some inattentive viewers, but not all. People in a state of deep inattention will most likely block it out. But providing it nonetheless helps many of the less inattentive, including the attentive viewers, receive your message easier and quicker.

- **Step 4: Repeat your company or product name many times in your audio track.** Television gives you the opportunity to make an impact on the brain from two directions at once, through the eyes and through the ears. Take advantage of the medium's double-barreled impact by delivering your company and/or product name in the audio track, either spoken or sung (jingles are a great simulconsciousing tool).

In many instances, an inattentive viewer may take his eyes off the screen completely during your commercial. He may even leave the room. But his subconscious mind is still susceptible to audio impact. During a recent football telecast I left the room to fetch something from the kitchen when a commercial came on (after I had viewed the first $1\frac{1}{2}$ seconds of it, by the way). During the time I was in the kitchen, I made a point of *consciously* listening to the television so as to make it back in time when the game returned. I was in the attentive state as far as the audio portion of the commercial was concerned. But what did I hear? Music. Nothing but music. No announcer, no singing, no words at all. Just unrecognizable music. Some marketer paid good money to reach people with this commercial, and I was obliging him by paying attention. I wanted to hear his message. But he failed to deliver it. Evidently he expected me to sit in front of the TV set and actually *watch* his commercial. What a disillusioned marketer.

Treating the audio strictly as support for the video is a big mistake. Treating the audio as if it were a radio commercial with no video at all is smart.

HOW TO SIMULCONSCIOUS YOUR RADIO COMMERCIALS

There is no other medium in which simulconsciousing is more important than radio. That's because radio listeners quite often use radio strictly as background sound, with no intent of ever paying conscious attention to it. Unlike watching television, when a person constantly shifts back and forth between the attentive and inattentive states, a radio listener may remain in the inattentive state for much longer periods of time.

Once you understand how to simulconscious in one medium, you'll pretty much know how to go about it in every medium. The principle is the same, regardless of medium. Here's how it works in radio.

Make sure your radio commercial contains the three simulconscious ad elements: your pre-processed word, product name, and point line. As in television, your pre-processed word and company or product name should be presented in the first $1\frac{1}{2}$

seconds. You accomplish most of your simulconsciousing by repeating your name many times throughout your commercial in a way that makes it stand out from the rest of the copy. Ott. Remember, it's good to have your company or product name simply pop up, or "hang" without any "justification" for its presence. Ott. You can accomplish this by simply dropping your product name in here and there, Ott, perhaps using another voice that simply states your name in between sentences of the primary voice. Or have a singing jingle, which repeats your name, running in the background. Ott. Or do it any other way you can think of. Ott. Get the idea?

In one 30-second commercial, your product name should be mentioned at least six times. Your point line should also be presented twice in a 30-second commercial, and four times in a 60-second commercial.

Remember, you can make an impact on the listener's brain even when it's in the inattentive state. But only the simple, straightforward simulconscious ad elements will make an impact. All that other wonderful, creative verbiage that one can understand only when paying attention will not make an impact on the inattentive listener.

HOW TO SIMULCONSCIOUS IN PRINT

Print includes newspaper and magazine ads, along with direct mail pieces and flyers. As long as you're at it, you may even want to simulconscious in your sales brochures.

I'm sure it comes as no surprise to you that not every person who sees a print ad reads every word of the copy. Your objective: Provide certain visual elements that catch the eye and make a subconscious impression, even if the person is consciously thinking of something else at the time. Here's where so many ad designers go wrong. The "eye catching" material they come up with ends up being a large photo or "clever" double-entendre, play-on-words headline of some kind. Then, after having presumably grabbed the reader's attention, they lead the reader along a winding road of equally "clever" copy, eventually getting around to making the point and presenting the company or product logo in the end (usually smallish and near the bottom of the ad).

Why try so hard to get the reader's attention, require her to spend her valuable time working her way through your copy, and only at the end get around to making the point you want her to get? That's like walking up to a stranger on the street, leading him off under your arm in another direction, and only eventually informing him why you're doing all of this. Wouldn't it make more sense simply to make the point at the very beginning, thereby leaving an impression whether or not he chooses to pay any further attention?

Although we do make specific design recommendations for our clients, I obviously can't recommend in this book how your ads, direct mail pieces, or brochures should be laid out. But I can tell you what you should emphasize, and you already know what that is. The simulconscious ad elements: your pre-processed word, logo, and point line. Big and bold. Any additional material is a bonus. If the reader wishes to stop and read further, fine. If he flips the page and moves on, you've made your point and left your impression.

HOW TO SIMULCONSCIOUS IN BILLBOARDS

You know enough about simulconsciousing now to tell me how to do it. Go ahead, tell me what a simulconscious billboard should look like.

In many cases, all you need on a billboard are two of your simulconscious ad elements, your pre-processed word and logo. In some cases, a point line is advantageous. And in some cases a phone number or location may also be appropriate. But don't have too many elements. I'll bet you've seen numerous billboards which contain so many visual elements you can't clearly read all the small writing or determine what they're trying to get across. Then again, perhaps you don't recall ever seeing such a billboard, which emphasizes my point. They exist, it's just that they make no impact.

UNINTENTIONAL SIMULCONSCIOUSING

Warning: You may be simulconsciousing your ads or commercials without even knowing you're doing it! And that can be very dangerous.

For example, Toshiba Copiers has a television commercial in which an office manager is so frustrated with his unreliable copier he dynamites it through the roof. What is on the television screen almost the entire 30 seconds? The problem copier. Then the Toshiba logo appears at the end of the commercial. To the attentive viewer, the message is clear: Replace your problem copier with a Toshiba (or avoid the headache and buy a Toshiba to begin with). But in the inattentive viewer's mind, two things may inadvertently become linked, the rotten copier and Toshiba. See the problem?

You also must be extremely cautious if you engage in any comparative advertising. When you show a competitor's product or logo, you're flirting with danger in an inattentive environment. While the attentive receiver may be able to grasp what you are saying, the inattentive receiver may only notice logo impressions ... your competitor's as well as yours.

When Pizza Hut decided to introduce its delivery service in a major way, it ran a television commercial showing people replacing their Domino's phone number with the Pizza Hut number. The original commercial also showed two Domino's delivery guys eating a Pizza Hut pizza for lunch. The commercial showed the Domino's logo almost as many times as the Pizza Hut logo. To the inattentive viewer, the Domino's logo made just as valid and positive an impression as the Pizza Hut logo. Inattentive viewers probably didn't know whether it was a Pizza Hut or Domino's commercial. They simply weren't paying enough attention to get anything but one or two simulconscious ad elements, Domino's as well as Pizza Hut's.

HAPPY SIMULCONSCIOUSING

The Simulconscious Strategy is not meant to limit creativity. If anything, it requires more creativity to construct an ad or commercial which appeals to two levels of consciousness instead of just one. Simulconsciousing is a form of creative discipline. It not only has the advantage of doubling the effectiveness of your advertising at no additional cost, but it keeps your advertising from becoming creatively impotent. Simulconsciousing forces your ad or commercial to be effective, regardless of all the other variables which go into the composition of each and every ad and commercial you craft.

The Simulconscious Strategy is a tool for you to use and enjoy. Have fun with it. Let it raise your advertising to a new level of creativity and effectiveness. Let it help your demand flourish.

PART 5

SUSTAINING DEMAND

I'll bet you've heard it said, "Getting to the top is easy, but staying there is the difficult part." While such an expression may keep the troops motivated after a victory, it certainly has no basis in reality. "Getting there" is definitely the difficult part. It's an upward struggle, requiring a great deal of dedication, energy, and perseverance, as well as the ability to take hits and recover from setbacks along the way. (Aren't you glad I didn't bring this up at the beginning of the book? You're in too deep to turn back now, pal.)

Standing on the mountain top is much easier than the climb it took to get there. Sustaining demand is much easier than creating it. That doesn't mean you can go on automatic pilot and take a nap. Remember prerequisite number one: You must adopt a marketing mindset. That is, you must continue to recognize the importance of marketing and continue to market wisely to sustain success. But unless you manage some major screw-ups (and you and I both know a number of people and companies that seem to display an amazing propensity to do so), you'll sustain demand just fine.

The first two chapters in this section are intended to help you keep demand strong and resilient. The remaining chapter will help prevent you from pulling the royal screw-up.

Chapter Twenty

The Art of Parlaying

I t takes a lot of fuel to get a jet off the ground and climbing. But once it has attained cruising altitude, it expends considerably less fuel continuing to streak through the sky at 500 miles an hour. At that point, it has *momentum*. The stronger your momentum, the greater the results you'll produce with any given level of effort.

One of the most effective ways to build marketing momentum is through the principle of *parlaying*. Parlaying uses the result of one action to pollinate subsequent actions. It means using one or more successful elements, or seeds, of each marketing activity (an ad, a promotion, a contest, or a publicity blurb) to launch other marketing activities. Let's look at an example.

PARLAYING EXAMPLE

Karen and Roxy own a flower shop. They participated in a weekend promotion organized by their shopping center's marketing department called "Fling Into Spring." All of the merchants in the center were to move some of their merchandise onto the sidewalk outside their doors and put particular items on sale for the weekend. The center's marketing department arranged for clowns, balloon decorations, and a horse-drawn carriage to give children rides around the parking lot. Karen and Roxy are expert parlayers. They know how to take the seeds from one success and grow subsequent successes. Here are some of the things they did to parlay the Fling Into Spring promotion.

First, they readied their 35-mm camera with fresh batteries and plenty of film. The shopping center had a photographer of its own working the event, but that didn't matter. Karen and Roxy knew the first rule of effective parlaying: Control the process. By taking their own photos, they controlled not only what appeared in the photos but also the subsequent use of the photos. After all, they would own them.

Second, they prepared their store. A number of signs were custom-made, featuring their logo, big and bold. Taking advantage of the fact that flowers, by nature, are visually beautiful, they doubled the usual number of arrangements in the store.

As any retailer knows, store traffic is extremely important. To ensure traffic, the women concocted a giveaway they called the "Free Love Weekend." All weekend long, they gave each and every male who entered their store a free long-stemmed rose so he could surprise his "special lady." They promoted the Free Love Weekend in their radio commercials starting 10 days before, and they put flyers on cars in the parking lot during the 3 days preceding. (The florists' Free Love Weekend occurred as part of the shopping center's Fling Into Spring . . . in other words, a promotion within a promotion.)

The Fling Into Spring promotion was a success, in terms of both sales and visibility. Here's how they parlayed its seeds into subsequent successes.

> *Seed:* A photo of a man presenting a rose to his wife (an unposed shot), amidst onlookers and the store's logo.
> *Subsequent action:* Newspaper publicity. Photos were sent to the local weekly newspaper. There was no guarantee the newspaper would run the photos, of course, but it cost practically nothing to send them. As it turned out, the newspaper ran one of the photos submitted, along with the caption submitted, in the paper's "Happening Around Town" feature.
> *Seed:* The newspaper photo.

Subsequent action: Milking the newspaper publicity. The newspaper photo was reprinted in a flyer mailed to people in the store's ever-growing database. The store owners had the article framed and have it hanging on the wall near the cash register.

Seed: Various photos of flowers and people inside and outside of the store.

Subsequent action: Sales material. A color brochure was printed using many of these photos. Karen and Roxy wanted to depict emotion in their brochure (in the form of happy people), and photos taken during this promotion's carnival atmosphere did the trick. After all, it's one thing to show flower arrangements, which of themselves have no emotional content, and quite another to show happy people gathered around touching and holding the flowers. People buzzing around the store also depicts demand. Such photos show that people want what these florists have to offer.

Seed: The Free Love Weekend rose giveaway.

Subsequent action: Building the in-house database. To receive his free rose, a man was asked to fill out a data card, including his name and address, plus the name of his "special lady" and her birthday and their wedding anniversary (if applicable). Needless to say, these men received "special reminders" in the mail at the appropriate times of year.

Seed: The Free Love Weekend rose giveaway.

Subsequent action: A spin-off version of the Free Love Weekend in which women received a free rose to present to their special man.

Karen and Roxy found no fewer than five different seeds which they parlayed into at least that many subsequent actions. And it all began with one basic promotional event.

PARLAY YOUR ADVERTISING

The preceding example showed you how a single promotional event can yield many seeds, and how those seeds can be parlayed into subsequent actions. But how do you parlay an advertisement or a commercial?

There are many ways. Here are a few.

- **Let one ad or commercial point to another.** Did you ever hear a radio commercial or see a television commercial that says, "See this Sunday's newspaper for details"? How about a newspaper ad that says to "Listen to WXXX for details"?
- **Cross-promote your media exposure.** There is a certain amount of prestige in having your ad appear in certain publications or your commercial run on certain radio and television stations. On your flyers, brochures, and print ads, put the words "As seen on WXXX television," (or heard on WXXX radio). In radio or television commercials, mention "As featured in The Anytown Gazette."
- **Create a celebrity through your advertising.** Give a person or mascot enough continual exposure in your advertising, and you've created a local celebrity. The opportunities to parlay a celebrity are endless. Your spokesperson or mascot can appear all over town at fundraising events, fairs, parades, speaking engagements, you name it. Every appearance he, she, or it makes is free advertising for you (not counting what it costs to pay your celebrity for his time).
- **Use reader info cards.** If you advertise in magazines, you're probably familiar with this one. Many magazines have "reader info cards" (or similar name) that allow the reader to circle numbers that correspond to ads throughout the issue. The reader mails the card to the magazine, and the magazine provides you with a list of the people who requested additional information about your product or service. You then contact these respondents with additional information, and of course, add their names to your database for ongoing follow-up.

CREATE PARLAY LOOPS

When you parlay the seed of one activity into another, then parlay the second activity back into the first, you've created a *parlay loop*. Here are some examples.

Recording artists loop quite often. They record an album, then go on tour. The album promotes the tour and the tour promotes the album. Then the loop itself can produce additional parlayable seeds. When the Rolling Stones did their Steel Wheels tour in 1990, they recorded it. In 1991, after the original *Steel Wheels* studio album had long since peaked in sales, a live album called *Flashpoint* from the tour recordings was released.

Authors and speakers are natural loopers. Speaking engagements promote books, and books promote speaking engagements.

You can use your ads, promotions, and contests to create loops. You direct-mail a contest flyer. Recipients enter by mailing the activator card back or bringing the card into your store and dropping it into an entry box. How do they win? By watching your subsequent ads or commercials to see if their name is mentioned, and calling your hotline within a specified time period after seeing their name.

Here's another possibility: You use your products or services as prizes in your contest. The prizes generate interest in the contest, and the contest acts as a conduit to distribute samples of your product or service, which in turn spurs sales.

The more you loop, the larger your loop becomes, like an expanding circle that reaches more and more people all the time.

FINANCIAL PARLAYING

There is another, less obvious aspect of parlaying that comes into play. In addition to parlaying seeds, you must parlay some of the *profits* from one action into subsequent actions. Karen and Roxy, for example, take some of the money they make from each promotion and put it into a "promotion fund" to bankroll future promotions. You really don't need a separate fund or account, although that's fine if you prefer. Mental allocation is adequate. Simply remember that some of the profits from your successes are needed to fuel subsequent successes, and provide accordingly.

In some cases, you may be ready to parlay your profits into another product or service. Put yourself in the place of Karen and Roxy for the moment. What can you do to parlay your retail floral business into a parallel profit center? Here's what Karen and Roxy did. They used the accumulated profits of their retail store to start a new division. The new division supplies and maintains flower arrangements at restaurants and hotels on a contract basis. The new division also works with professional decorators to supply arrangements to their clients as needed. The cash the women injected into this division was used to hire extra help, install and maintain a separate phone line, and market the service aggressively.

The worst thing you can do with your profits is to squander them on things that consume cash and produce nothing in return. The next worst thing you can do is to hoard inordinate amounts of cash. While it's always wise to keep some cash in reserve, even a large amount can evaporate rapidly in times of need and leave you with nothing. The best move is to parlay your accumulated earnings into other profit centers that produce new revenue. Notice I didn't say you should speculate. Nor do I necessarily mean you should diversify. Speculation and diversification get many businesspeople into trouble quite often because they end up in areas they know little or nothing about. Always start with your area of expertise and seek new or different markets you can move into.

HOW TO BECOME A PARLAY ARTIST

As the title of this chapter indicates, successful parlaying is an art, an art you can become proficient at. The following tips will help you to parlay effectively.

- **Learn to recognize seeds.** There is always at least one seed from every marketing action you undertake that can be parlayed into another action. Often there is more than one element you can parlay. The secret is recognizing each of them. You'll get better at spotting seeds as you gain parlaying experience.
- **Think creatively.** The more creative you become, the more seeds you can find and the more subsequent actions they can initiate.
- **Take control.** Certainly some good things happen as natural consequences of your marketing activity. But many more

good things happen when you take control and make them happen.

- **Parlay constantly.** You don't gain momentum by parlaying once in a while. Parlaying should be something you do all the time, as standard procedure.

Chapter Twenty-one

Maintaining Demand through Reinforcement

A funny thing happens after people buy your product or service. They begin to doubt their decision. They may not show it openly. They may not even admit it to themselves. But somewhere in the backs of their minds, they're asking themselves if they made the right decision. The question is not whether a person has some doubt about a purchase decision. A person always has some doubt. The pertinent question is, "How strong is the doubt?" Doubt and belief are complementary parts of a whole and are inversely related. If belief is 99 percent, then doubt is one percent. If belief is 40 percent, doubt is 60 percent.

When doubt becomes stronger than belief, the scales tip and people take action. They may return the product, or cancel your services. They may bad-mouth you whenever the opportunity to do so arises. They may even sue you or stir up some negative publicity. And, needless to say, a repeat purchase is totally out of the question.

Since repeat business from happy customers is critical in demand creation, you must take deliberate measures to squelch doubt and keep it at an innocuous level. This doubt-squelching process is called *reinforcement*. When you reinforce the purchase decision, you're immunizing your customers against the growth of doubt. At the same time, you're creating the right mental condition for repeat business, and that in turn allows you to encourage endorsement successfully. When you make reinforcement a regular part of your marketing program, you'll keep demand pumping harder and longer.

WHY DOUBT EXISTS

Doubt is a fungus that multiplies when the conditions are right. The conditions that cause doubt to grow are *blurred judgment, different expectations,* and *competitive propaganda.*

1. Many people are simply unable to judge the benefits or results of a product or service accurately. If your company refinishes the hardwood floors in my house, how do I know if you've done a really good job? The floors may look shiny, but how do I know whether they're not supposed to look twice as shiny? How do I know you didn't use some cheap solution that will ruin the wood within a month? How do I know some other company wouldn't have done a better job at half the price?

   People may lack the necessary knowledge or experience to determine whether your product is performing exactly as it should. We call this condition blurred judgment. And the blurrier their judgment is, the more doubt they have.

2. The second condition that nurtures doubt is different expectations. For any number of possible reasons, a person may have been under the impression that your product or service would perform differently from what it actually does. The item in question may be performing perfectly well, but if the buyer had different expectations, doubt about the purchase grows.

3. Competitive propaganda also fosters the growth of doubt. Remember, your competitors' marketing messages will reach your customers. Some of those messages may be very persuasive. The more a competitor's bug swirls around in a person's mind, the more the person doubts he made the right decision in purchasing your item.

REINFORCE AFTER EVERY PURCHASE

After people make a purchase decision, their brains seek reinforcement. That is, they want to receive subsequent information that supports their purchase. Accordingly, there's an open door to the person's brain which someone—let us hope you—will step through and deliver the needed reinforcement.

When you supply the reinforcement the person seeks, you squelch doubt and avoid its nasty ramifications. What happens if you don't supply reinforcement? Your customer will likely get it from other sources. Guess what? One of those sources may very well be one of your competitors. And you can bet that type of reinforcement will be doubt-provoking rather than doubt-squelching.

TWO TYPES OF REINFORCEMENT

Reinforcement can be of two varieties, *internal* or *external*.

Internal reinforcement comes from the actual performance or results of the product or service itself. For example, your new lawnmower starts on the first pull and cuts well. Or the restaurant you've chosen serves you a great-tasting club sandwich.

External reinforcement comes from any source other than the product or service itself. Perhaps your new lawnmower received an excellent rating in a *Consumer Reports* article. Or the friend you're having lunch with remarks how great his club sandwich tastes. External reinforcement can even come from the marketer of the product or service in question. Any reinforcement except that which the product's or service's actual performance provides is external.

I've got a question for you. Which type of reinforcement, internal or external, is stronger? Which has the bigger effect on people? For most people, most of the time, external reinforcement is much stronger. That is, the actual performance of your product or service, as good as it may be, may not be enough to keep doubt in remission. You must deliberately reinforce, or doubt can grow regardless of how well your product or service performs.

HOW TO REINFORCE THE PURCHASE DECISION

- **Step 1: Give the consumer more than he expected.** If your package says it contains 16 ounces, make sure it actually contains 16.5 or 17 ounces. If your package of baseball cards says there are 14 in the pack, put 15 in there. If you agreed to finish a job on the 18th of the month, finish it on the 15th. If someone buys x number of kloptigobinators, deliver x plus a few extras.

  The idea is to nip doubt in the bud by making a positive and *unexpected* impression at the time the buyer takes possession of your product or service. The key to making this work is that it must be unexpected. The buyer must be surprised that he got more than he paid for. If you hype your extra whatever before the purchase ("Buy 14 . . . get one more free!") then the buyer expects the extra and its reinforcing ability has been negated.

  I'm not saying you shouldn't package things creatively and hype the deal. I am saying such is not reinforcement. Packaging and hyping are great; reinforcing by surprising the buyer with more than he expected is great. But the two techniques are not the same thing. Do both.

- **Step 2: Provide belief-raising, doubt-reducing information.** Address each of the doubt-breeding conditions: blurred judgment, higher expectations, and competitive propaganda. Educate people on the proper ways to judge results. Tell them exactly what to expect. Assure them they have gotten a quality item at a good price.

  Hammer home your reinforcing copy by repeating it often. Like telling your spouse you love him or her, once may not be enough. People need a steady dose of reinforcement to keep their positive feelings alive.

  Testimonial statements from other satisfied customers are strong reinforcers. People don't always trust their own judgment. But seeing or hearing other people express satisfaction tends to cause similar thinking in themselves.

- **Step 3: Reinforce in your advertising.** Your advertising is not intended just to persuade new customers to buy. It's also intended to reinforce your present or past customers. Did you ever notice you pay greater attention to an ad or commercial *after* you purchased the product or service advertised? That's because your subconscious mind is looking for reinforcement.

AT&T's slogan, "AT&T. The Right Choice," is the best use of reinforcement in advertising I've ever seen. In fact, AT&T reinforces not only in its slogan, but throughout much of its ad copy. The next time you see an AT&T ad or commercial, take note. You'll see or hear quite a few reinforcing statements throughout.

- **Step 4: Reinforce in written material.** Written sales material is supplied before the purchase, written reinforcing material is to be supplied after the purchase. And the reinforcing material should not be a rehashed version of the sales material. Your reinforcement material should give the buyer something more, something she hasn't seen before. Make it a pleasant surprise.

Remember when your company refinished my floors and I harbored doubts about your work? Do you think my doubts would have diminished if, after I had signed the work order, you provided me with a brochure explaining how the process works, how to judge results, and how long I should expect my shiny new floor to last? And would my doubts have diminished even further if, upon completing the work, you handed me yet another printed piece guaranteeing the work and supplying me with a special phone number to call if I had any further questions or comments?

How about sending some reinforcing material to people after they have mailed in their warranty registration card? Isn't it odd how each of us receives a ton of literature before the purchase, but little or none after? You feel the marketer abandons you right after you've decided to embrace him. That's not a good feeling. To avoid that problem, each time another warranty card comes in, add the name to your database of buyers. Work those people! Make them customers for life by constant reinforcement.

Chapter Twenty-two
Preventing Demand Disintegration

D emand doesn't increase forever. Eventually demand will level off somewhat; things will slow down. It's one of the natural laws of the universe, and there's nothing you can do to alter that.

However, there are things you can do to cause demand to level off much sooner than it otherwise might. In fact, there are things you can do that actually cause demand to screech to a halt. All of these things fall under the heading of screwing up. Believe me, no matter how high your demand jet is flying at the moment, it can come crashing down in no time if you screw up big enough.

Of all the pitfalls out there, there are only five that are lethal enough to destroy you. To guard against their clutches, you must recognize them, then defend yourself against them. Otherwise, there's a good chance you'll fall victim sooner or later. Take note, and take precautions.

PITFALL NUMBER ONE: THE DOWNWARD SPIRAL

As I stated, demand doesn't grow forever. A number of factors can cause your demand to sputter at times. A new competitor pops up, the economy tightens, a piece of bad publicity bites, or your product simply reaches maturity. The question is not why or even when demand will slow down, but *how you react to the slowdown* when it arrives.

An all-too-common pitfall that destroys many marketers is called the *downward spiral trap*. Here's the lethal scenario. As demand slows and revenues decline, profit margins are squeezed. Once you've become accustomed to a particular profit margin and planned your budgets accordingly, it's extremely difficult to accept any less. So the marketer adjusts in a logical way; that is, he cuts expenses. The area that almost always gets cut first is marketing. In accounting parlance, advertising and promotion are referred to as "discretionary expenses," meaning they can be reduced or cut without adversely affecting operations.

The accountants are partly right. Under certain conditions, you can reduce your marketing expenses and suffer few harmful results in the short run. The effect is called *coasting*. It is analogous to the pilot of a jet pulling back on the throttle. The jet still streaks through the sky, its momentum propelling it along as though no cutback occurred.

With momentum, your revenues can often be maintained for a while even though you cut back on your marketing throttle. In other words, because of momentum, there's a time lag between the reduction in your marketing activity and the decline of your revenues. This lag can create the false impression that a healthy amount of marketing is not necessary. As time goes on, however, your momentum slows and the time lag runs out. Revenues now indeed begin to fall.

As revenues decrease further in our scenario, the marketer adjusts by cutting marketing budgets further. Since the time lag that once existed between reduced marketing activity and ensuing demand reduction has long since evaporated, an immediate decline in revenue results. The marketer reacts by cutting marketing back further. The process repeats until revenue, and demand, have fallen below the point of no return.

Once you are caught in the downward spiral, it's almost impossible to get out. A tremendous amount of marketing power is required to reverse your downward fall and climb back to the level you once had. The odds of pulling your demand jet out of its tailspin are overwhelmingly against you.

The only way to survive the downward spiral is to avoid getting caught in it in the first place. You must maintain marketing expenditures through good times and bad. If you must reduce your marketing expenditures and coast at certain times, do so only for brief interludes. You must throttle-up quickly before revenues begin to decline.

PITFALL NUMBER TWO: COMPETITOR FIXATION

Have you noticed that until now, I haven't really spoken much about competition? Except for our discussion of how to instigate shunning in Chapter 16, this tip-and-tactic marketing book offers no other tips or tactics designed to help you thwart a competitor. Why? Simple. Too many marketers spend too much time worrying too much about what their competitors are doing instead of concentrating on what they themselves are doing. In fact, many marketers become so obsessed with their competitors that they really have no idea what it is they themselves are doing. Paying an inordinate amount of attention to a competitor is called *competitor fixation*. It's a condition you want to avoid.

Does this mean you should ignore your competitors? Of course not. It's obvious you must be constantly aware of what any and all competitors are doing, and consider all relevant information in your decisions. You should also keep up with any technological and marketing advances that a competitor makes. Other than that, don't worry about them! They're going to do what's best for them, and you must do what's best for you. You've got to keep your eye on the ball—your consumers or customers—and not have your attention diverted by a dazzling or taunting competitor, especially a weak one.

Victims of fixation lose their ability to think rationally. Rather than looking after themselves, they end up making decisions designed primarily to thwart a competitor (the two are rarely one and the same, despite any illusion). They become so caught up in this "killer mentality," they live for bashing the competition in every way possible. Many victims of fixation fail to keep their thwarting efforts above-board and ethical, unfortunately for everyone concerned.

The truth is, your competitors will more often than not suffer as a result of your successful marketing moves anyway. You don't need to expend undue energy trying to inflict pain on them, especially if they lack one or more of the prerequisites of success. Besides, the idea is to suck your competitors into fixating on you, not the other way around. Once they begin stalking you and reacting to your every move, you know you've got 'em. Just continue to do what's best for you and your customers, and let the competition continue to follow you around like a dog does its master.

Take Sam Walton as an example. The founder of Wal-Mart will occasionally walk into a competing store and check it out. He takes notes, evaluates what he sees, even gets an idea or two. But that's about it. In 1990 Wal-Mart surpassed Sears as the number one retailer in the United States, and *USA Today* asked Sam for a comment on the triumph. "We're not in the business to beat Sears," he stated. Beating Sears was never a goal at Wal-Mart. Its goal was to serve its customers as best it could, and let the competitive situation take care of itself. Amen.

Remember this: Marketing is not a war game between you and your competitors. It is a romance between you and your consumers. Reward comes not from killing the competition, but from attracting the consumer. If you make decisions in this light, you'll avoid the pitfalls of fixation.

PITFALL NUMBER THREE: INTERNAL STRIFE

Like pitfall number one, this pitfall is an inappropriate reaction to a natural slowdown or glitch in demand and revenues.

When revenues slow down, people within an organization often panic. They start questioning the very things that made them successful. They start doubting their own moves. They begin arguing among themselves, often creating internal turmoil that renders their future marketing moves weak and ineffective. They fall victim to the pitfall of *internal strife*.

Internal strife is a cancer that weakens and eventually kills you. It's caused by people within an organization who continually question and doubt their own marketing program. Even one doubter can cause constant conflict, ultimately weakening the organization to the point of inhibiting success.

There is a time and place for dissent and disagreement. That time is before you put a particular plan into effect, before the action starts. For example, the United States Congress debated whether President Bush should have the authority to commit American troops to battle in the Persian Gulf in early 1991. Once every member of Congress had a chance to speak his or her mind, and once the vote was taken, debate stopped. Congress then backed the president and the troops with unwavering commitment.

Not every marketing move you make will be successful. You will suffer marketing setbacks at times. The question is, will you remain committed, focused, harmonious, and strong... or will you question, doubt, argue, and buckle?

PITFALL NUMBER FOUR: FAILURE TO REINVEST

At last, demand for your kloptigobinators is at stratospheric height and the money's rolling in. Now you're in the position to do what you've always dreamed of. In rapid succession you move the company into the stateliest of quarters, purchase a fleet of automobiles for your top managers, acquire an unrelated business, and hire a contingent of secretaries for your secretaries. Likewise, you make magnificent additions to your personal antique car, yacht, and Asian art collections. In short, you do everything with the profits except reinvest in the product or service that produced the profit.

People are entitled to indulge in the rewards of their labor, no doubt. But a person shouldn't starve the golden goose to death in the process. Any successful product or service will remain successful only through constant reinvestment. These products or services must have some of the cash they produce returned to them to maintain success. In fact, they should receive increased budgets for product improvement and marketing, not less. Yet too many products, services, and entire businesses are allowed to weaken or die because the marketer siphons off all the profits. I'll bet you can name at least one person who milked his company for all he could, invested in some nonrelated pet project that ate cash and returned nothing, and ended up not only killing the business, but running for cover in bankruptcy court.

Your successful product or service requires a constant supply of cash reinvestment to keep it alive and healthy. Avoiding the *failure to reinvest* pitfall is simply a matter of keeping the golden goose properly fed.

PITFALL NUMBER FIVE: HUBRIS

Ask anyone who has had his or her once high-flying success crumble to nothing what the lesson of this experience has been, and chances are the answer will be "humility."

You don't have to learn the hard way. While your business is still thriving, take a moment to recognize a few realities. Recognize that some of your success is due to sheer luck. Recognize that success in one area or endeavor is not always easily repeated in another. Recognize that things totally outside your control can come along and have a major adverse effect on you at any time. Laws change, people die, technology advances, products and services fall in and out of favor, the economy tightens, catastrophes occur. Anything can happen.

Be grateful for what you have. Share your success with others. Recognize and reward the people who consistently contribute to your success. In short, carry a tad of humility rather than hubris with you. When you do, your chances of maintaining success over the long run are much greater.

PART 6

GETTING HELP

Who will do all your marketing strategizing, planning, creating, and executing? Besides you and/or any number of people in your organization, you'll most likely require some form of outside help. Marketing is just too important to go it alone.

Help can come from any number of sources, including consultants, researchers, and production houses that specialize in specific media such as television commercials or direct mail campaigns. The most common source of help is obviously the advertising agency. Most readers of this book will have an agency. The first chapter in this part is designed to help you get the most from your agency . . . to help them help you succeed.

The final chapter is designed to help you help yourself succeed. You'll learn about the one key ingredient that is necessary to make all you've read about thus far effective.

Chapter Twenty-three
The Truth about Ad Agencies

T he truth is, there are a number of very good people doing some very good work at some very good ad agencies. The truth is, a good agency will help you much more than it'll hurt you.

So why is there such an abundance of mediocre, even down-right terrible, advertising out there? With all this good quality going in—the people, the work, and the agencies—you'd expect better quality coming out, wouldn't you? Something is amiss. Let's determine exactly where the problem lies so you can guard against its consequences.

FLAWS IN THE AGENCY SYSTEM

All fingers point to the system under which advertising agencies, and their clients, operate. Specifically, there are three fundamental flaws in the system.

Flaw Number One: Account Pitching.

Agencies must spend a big chunk of time and energy creating *pro forma* campaigns for accounts they hope to "win." (An "account," from an agency's perspective, is a product or service with an advertising budget.) That is, they must arrive at your door with a well-defined strategy and campaign—two elements of vital importance—already completed just to make an appeal for your business.

Wouldn't all the time and energy an agency spends on account pitching be better spent serving its existing accounts instead? Absolutely! And the agencies are the first to admit it. If there were a way around having to concoct elaborate, sometimes exotic, pitches to secure new accounts, agencies would rejoice.

Clients, on the other hand, love to be pitched. They've long since discovered that the utterance of three magic words, "up for review," instantly produces a hoard of salivating agencies panting at the door. The client (or potential client, as the case may be) extends "offers to pitch" to a number of interested agencies, each of which then dives into grindstone mode and comes up with a strategy and campaign (never in haste, of course). The real fun starts when each agency, pressure-pitted against the others, delivers its song and dance to a group of reveling executives comfortably perched on their thrones of power, hooting and howling between swigs of spirited libation.

Under this system, hiring an ad agency has degenerated into a contest. Do you really believe this pitching process results in a higher caliber of work that will benefit you, the client? If so, then you may as well hire your medical doctor, legal counsel, and accounting firm the same way. "But it's not done that way in those industries," you point out. Ah, perhaps there is a good reason.

Flaw Number Two: Award-Winning Mentality

Human nature dictates that we all want appreciation and recognition. The ego-intensive advertising business is no exception. (Healthy egos, by the way, are not necessarily a negative. Often the people with the biggest egos turn out the best work.)

Embedded in the depths of every advertising person's mind is an ever-present, unquenchable desire to create advertising that wins awards. (In some agencies, the objective is not far from the surface.) It's almost impossible to operate otherwise in such an award-conscious industry.

This would be fine if the award-winning advertising were the same as the sales-generating advertising. The truth is, however, that what wins awards often does not sell product. In fact, the ads and commercials that win the major awards are often the biggest failures in terms of affecting sales of the products or services they're supposed to be promoting. Many marketers are surprised—sometimes shocked—to find out that the criteria for determining award-worthy advertising have *nothing to do with the sales results of the product or service in question.*

Agencies design advertising to win awards because that's where the recognition comes from. The alternative is to create advertising that has no chance of ever winning an award. Wisk's long-running "Ring Around The Collar" campaign is a classic example. It is an artistic dud by any award-determining criterion, but it sells loads of Wisk.

But when a campaign results in extraordinary sales, the client invariably takes all the credit. Mushrooming sales must be due to the superiority of the product or service, or to the client's intelligence, right? As for the ad agency, their reward is to keep the account for a while longer. But recognition? What recognition? No wonder agencies look beyond sales results for reward.

Flaw Number Three: The Client-As-Expert Mentality

It's not commonly expressed outside the advertising fraternity, but if you could ask an agency off the record what its biggest obstacle usually is, chances are it would tell you it's their clients themselves. And that's if you talk to account executives, who are generally very diplomatic people. Talk to creative people and you'll hear roaring horror stories about how their entire work has been so mangled and mutilated by clients that they couldn't even recognize it in the end.

Not that agencies are always right and their clients are always wrong. Each party is likely right only half the time. Probably you know more about your business than any agency will ever know, and your agency knows more about advertising than you'll ever know. This makes a strong argument for a client-agency relationship built on collaboration and decisions by consensus.

But a funny thing happens to people when they start dealing with advertising. The same person who believes he needs outside expertise in the areas of medicine, law, or accounting for some reason believes he possesses all the expertise necessary when it comes to advertising. Since marketers of this mindset believe they know how their advertising should be done, they view their agency not as collaborators, but merely as executors. Their personal objective is to see that the agency simply carries out their orders. As you might expect, the result most often is an ineffectual piece of advertising mediocrity.

HOW TO GET THE MOST OUT OF YOUR AGENCY

You suffer from the system only if you abide by the system. There are no laws forcing you to do so in advertising. You, the client, have the power to operate differently, and you don't have to single-handedly spearhead a movement to revolutionize the entire advertising industry to do so. Simply do what's best for you, and forget about how everyone else chooses to operate.

Here are my recommendations for choosing an agency.

- **Step 1: Narrow down your choice of agencies to two or three before contacting them.** Choose agencies whose work you admire. If they've demonstrated ability and skill under varying circumstances for other clients, chances are they can do the same for you. Don't rule out new agencies, either. Although they may not have a track record of success to show, they may make up for it in enthusiasm, desire, and talent. Your account may be more important to them than it would be to a larger, established agency (this is especially true if you are a rather small account). You can locate new agencies simply by calling your local advertising club.

- **Step 2: Interview your two or three choices.** Don't get caught up in agency pitches. Instead, meet with each of your choices and start a discussion. Tell them a little about your business and what you're trying to accomplish. See how well they listen. Ask a number of questions about their philosophies and working methods. But don't put them in a position of having to offer specific advice about your situation. You haven't engaged their services yet, so don't expect them to come up with any answers yet. Although you may need more than one meeting, one agency will soon distinguish itself from the others, for whatever reasons.

Here are some tips for working with your agency, in no particular order.

• **Offer recognition.** Share your success with your agency. The way(s) you choose to demonstrate your appreciation can be many and varied. Here are some possibilities:

Mention its name when you're interviewed by the press about your success.

Why not give the agency your own award? How many agencies get to show prospective clients an award it's earned from an existing client? That's a major credibility booster any agency will cherish. (At the same time, let them know you will become suspicious of their work if it wins any award other than your own.)

Allow your agency to cite the sales results of your product or service as evidence of their fine work.

Do you pay your agency a bonus based on predetermined levels of sales achieved?

Do you invite your agency people to any of your staff parties?

Ninety-nine percent of all clients fail to offer their agency any recognition or reward beyond simply paying their bills, and many clients are slow to do even that. Herein lies a major opportunity for you. If you do the opposite, and offer recognition and reward, you can become the dream client every agency hopes to find some day. On which account do you think your agency will want to spend most of their time and effort yours or the other 99 percent who don't show any appreciation?

- **Don't meddle.** Recognize from the first that the people at your agency are well-versed in the ways of advertising. I doubt you'd commission an artist to paint your portrait and then stand over his shoulder and tell him how to paint. Don't hire an ad agency and then tell them how to do their job. That's not to say you shouldn't be communicating with your agency. Your opinions are valuable, and your agency needs to hear them. As I said earlier, collaborate and arrive at consensus decisions. But once those agreements have been made, get out of the way and let your agency do its job.

- **Be honest and eliminate surprises.** Let your agency know from the outset whether you want to stick with proven, established concepts or whether you're ready for an adventurous, experimental approach. And be honest. It's amazing how often clients will say they're ready to "blow it wide open" and "shake some trees," only to fearfully backpedal after the agency has worked hard and long to create a campaign that does exactly that.

- **If you've got a case of Gotta-Change-Something Disease, shake it.** Marketers afflicted with this disease feel compelled to demand at least one change in everything they see, regardless of merit. The primary symptoms are comments like these:

    "The commercial is fine, but I don't like the actor."

    "Make the picture bigger and the type smaller."

    "The woman should be wearing a green dress, not a red dress."

    "The (fill in the blank) is okay, but the (fill in the blank) has got to go."

People display Gotta-Change-Something Disease because they subconsciously feel a need to affirm their position and flex their authority. Secure, self-assured people aren't afflicted. They know they get the best work out of their agency by displaying trust in their agency's judgment, not by displaying doubt through token changes. (Of course, an error or technical mistake always deserves correction.)

Chapter Twenty-four

The Key Ingredient That Makes It All Work

H uman nature is human nature. The human brain works today the same as it has since the beginning of humanity and
is unlikely to change. That's why the material in this book works
so well. All of the tips, tactics, strategies, and techniques I've de-
scribed are based on immutable principles of human psychology,
principles that I did not invent or discover. I merely analyzed
them and found ways in which they can be used to market effectively. Therefore, except for a few small tidbits, the material in
this book is timeless. It will work for you today as well as at any
time in the future.

But there is one major ingredient missing, an ingredient so important and necessary that without it, none of the material in this
book is likely to work for you. I would gladly have supplied this
marvelous ingredient if I were able, but I can't. The only person
who can supply the missing, magical ingredient is you. Your *brain
power*—your *creativity* and *ideas*—is the invaluable ingredient that
activates the strategies and techniques and makes them work.

As I said in the preface, one of my goals was to get you
thinking . . . to stimulate your mind as you read. Now that you've

finished the book, I want to take one more step and challenge you. I want to challenge you to create ways of implementing all you've learned in *Creating Demand*. To take this material and mold it to your individual situation in unique and different ways.

In addition, I challenge you to use this book as a springboard to tap into many other strategies and techniques that we haven't discussed. Use this material as you would a chemistry set. Experiment. Discover. Create. By doing so, you'll realize not only massive demand for your product or service, but a whole new level of accomplishment and reward for yourself in the process.

Index

OTHER BUSINESS ONE IRWIN TITLES OF INTEREST TO YOU

THE UNITED STATES MAIL ORDER INDUSTRY
A Maxwell Sroge Report

Details how technologies, strategies, and postal increases are affecting the mail order business' growth. Analyzes performances of the top 25 consumer and business-to-business firms to help direct-marketing professionals, investors, and entrepreneurs find profitable market niches, project probable growth patterns, and allocate valuable marketing resources more accurately.
1-55623-486-4 $55.00

THE NEW DIRECT MARKETING
How to Implement a Profit-Driven Database Marketing Strategy
David Shepard Associates

Construct, analyze, use, and evaluate the information in a marketing database to build sales and profits. The authors show you how to cost-effectively acquire the primary and secondary data you need to identify and profile your best customers and prospects.
1-55623-317-5 $52.50

SELLING TO THE AFFLUENT
The Professional's Guide to Closing the Sales that Count
Dr. Thomas J. Stanley

Improve your closing percentage . . . and income. Dr. Stanley shows you how to approach wealthy prospects at the moment they are most likely to buy. In *Marketing to the Affluent*, Stanley tells you how to find them. Here he tells you how to sell them.
1-55623-418-X $55.00

MARKETING TO THE AFFLUENT
Dr. Thomas J. Stanley

A 1989 business book award finalist! Dr. Stanley shows you how to get the true demographics, psychographics, buying and patronage habits of the wealthy. Includes in-depth interviews with some of the nation's top sales and marketing professionals to help you pinpoint your best prospects.
1-55623-105-9 $55.00

ADVERTISING AGENCY MANAGEMENT
Jay McNamara, former president, McCann-Erickson Worldwide

"Jay McNamara has concisely and comprehensively compiled in one volume what every aspiring agency manager should be learning on the way up and what no advertising manager should ever forget after he or she gets there."
Allen Rosenshine, Chairman and CEO, BBDO Worldwide Inc.
1-55623-230-6 $29.95

Prices quoted are in U.S. currency and are subject to change without notice.
Available in fine bookstores and libraries everywhere.